GROW WITH ME

Dr. Lisa L. Campbell®

McClure Publishing, Inc.

Lisa L. Campbell © Copyright - McClure Publishing, Inc.

All rights reserved. Printed and bound in the United States of America. According to the 1976 United States Copyright Act. No part of this book may be reproduced or utilized in any form or by any means, electronic or mechanical, including photocopying, recording, or by any information storage or retrieval system, except by a reviewer who may quote brief passages in a review to be printed in a magazine or newspaper, without permission in writing from the Publisher: Inquiries should be addressed to McClure Publishing, Inc. Permissions Department, 398 West Army Trail Road, #124, Bloomingdale, Illinois 60108. Publication date: August 5, 2023.

The author and publisher have made every effort to ensure the accuracy and completeness of information contained in this book. We assume no responsibility for errors, inaccuracies, omissions, or any inconsistencies therein.

Any slights of people, places, belief systems or organizations are unintentional. Any resemblance to anyone living, dead or somewhere in between is truly coincidental.

ISBN 13: 979-8-9877802-2-0

Cover Design and Interior Layout by Kathy McClure
https://McClurePublishing.com

Order additional copies, please contact
books@mcclurepublishing.com
800.659.4908

~~~

Consulting Services and Speaking Engagements Contact:
Dr. Lisa L. Campbell
www.DrLisaLCampbell.org
drlisa@drlisalcampbell.org
855.737.5472

Professional Photographs
Jason McCoy Photography
www.JasonMcCoyPhotography.com

Professional Stylist
Brandon K. Momon
www.StyleMeBrandon.com

I dedicate this book to my daughter Jasmine!

You have impacted me in so many ways, my sweet princess!

Table of Contents

Page

Introduction

Chapter One 15
    Life Challenges

Chapter Two 33
    The Education Journey

Chapter Three 57
    Jasmine

Chapter Four 71
    The House The Campbells Built

Chapter Five 83
    You Work Too Much

Chapter Six 95
    They Don't Know Me Or My Journey

Chapter Seven 99
    Weight And The Wait

Chapter Eight 105
    The Village

Chapter Nine 117
    A Slaughter WOMAN

Chapter Ten 121
    The Birth of the Growth Motivator

Chapter Eleven 127
    The Growth Community

Chapter Twelve 149
   Faith Over Fear
        Biography of Dr. Lisa L. Campbell
        SYNPOSIS: GROW With Me

Introduction

This motivational book is about 50 years of WEIGHT! Now, I know what you are thinking! No, this book is not about dieting, healthy eating, exercise, and my journey toward becoming a smaller version of myself! There are enough books on the market for that. Plus, if you noticed on the front cover, I am not that small, but I am happy, exercise on a regular basis, and monitor my food intake.

Additionally, if you ever have an opportunity to meet me. I am generally smiling and full of energy because my "Shed the Weight™" journey has established me as The Growth Motivator™, where I help individuals and businesses in all industries shed excess baggage and develop growth mindsets that allow them to live life without regrets!

Many people think that I am impatient, and when I want something, I want it now. Further, I'm not willing to WAIT! Those who know me understand that my excitement means I have thought about it. I am ready to execute it! I am a trailblazer, a thinker, and a visionary who knows where I have been and operates with purpose. In other words, hashtag, I know my assignment! I don't need direction, nor do I need a director to assist me with leading the way. I am self-motivated! But to be clear, having a coach and therapist has helped me soar!

For example, in 1978, one sunny afternoon, I was waiting on my father, Edward, Jr., to pick me up from kindergarten. On that day, he was nowhere to be found! He never showed up. I had to make a decision. I was not afraid. Inside of me was a mechanism that always get to the solution even at that young age.

Fear is a learned behavior. As we grow, we take less risk. WEIGHT keeps many of us from reaching our true potential. The skills we are born with sit on the shelf and need more space to cultivate. Instead, we spend time WAITING and hoping for the best! I've done this my entire life.

Here are a few examples:

I waited seven years for my daughter to walk, while most children walk in one year or less.

I waited thirty-nine years to get married while I watched my friends get married in their twenties.

I waited nine years to complete my doctoral degree, while my classmates finished in four.

I waited twenty-one years to become a full-time entrepreneur.

Transitioning to entrepreneurship full-time becomes the impetus for this book! All it took was one disrespectful email from a new manager at a university where I was employed full-time! I waited to become a full-time entrepreneur primarily because of fear. Until my Certified Public Accountant (CPA) and friend Kristal Stevenson said, "Sis, you should execute "faith over fear." I took a leap of faith and decided to Shed the WEIGHT™ I was carrying! I was no longer going to be held hostage by Salary and Benefits!

While I was working full-time at a university remotely working on growing my consulting business Physician Practice Resources, Inc., there was a change in the leadership. The person who had motivated everyone else, who had given their all to everyone, a high performer, had been disrespected and undervalued and decided that the WAIT was over! After discussing it with my husband, praying, screaming, and crying, I decided that I would resign shortly after my 50th birthday and not look back!

We all carry barrels of WEIGHT as humans. It doesn't matter our nationality, race, gender, sexual orientation, or age. The pandemic, mass shootings, and civil unrest have demonstrated that no one is exempt from carrying heavy WEIGHT. I decided that in the next 50 years on my journey of this precious life, I will walk in my Zone of Genius. I will inspire individuals to drop the WEIGHT holding them back! Whatever that WEIGHT is for them.

A few months before my 50th birthday, I started working out with a personal trainer LaRon of Body by LaRon. You know how the saying goes that the world gets smaller and smaller. It was interesting the connection that LaRon, and I had. His cousin Sasha was in the Modeling Club with me, one of the activities I participated in while attending Fenger High School, located on the Southside of Chicago.

For the first time in a long time, I thought about using my influence to inspire young girls and women about the importance of looking and feeling good from the inside out! Now I know what you are thinking; she said this book was not about WEIGHT! It is not. I hired a personal trainer, but I was not too fond of how my legs looked around my knees, and I decided to do something about it. No one had ever said anything about them, at least not to my face!

When I started my "Body by LaRon" journey in November 2022, I am not going to lie; it was hard because I was so used to doing a cardio-only fitness routine, not consistently. I could be better. Weight training, ropes, burpees, leg presses, and all the other things I do three days per week, I was thinking, I am too old to become a bodybuilder. I want to tone my legs and avoid those statins, lol!

However, when February 2023 rolled around, and I was preparing to take my pictures for the cover of this book, I could see the results. I saw myself on the stage in front of thousands of people giving my signature speech, Shed the Weight™ thanks to Ashley, Chris, and my Speak Your Way to Cash® (SYWTC) community.

I've been speaking on numerous stages since 2003, but the scene in my dream was larger than life! When I walked out on stage, this time was different! I felt and looked different. I am no longer held hostage by "WEIGHT". I immediately got extra excited and have been fixated on my legs because I have nice legs that need some shaping! Don't worry, hubby; I belong to you!

You must admit, the cover photo is terrific! I can hear my auntie Debra Slaughter right now; girl, you are so vain! My photographer Jason McCoy is the best in the business! Oh, yeah, and my stylist Brandon had selected color patterns that made me uneasy for weeks before the photoshoot. Now before you think, is she rich? Nope, not at all, I struggled to pay for the photo shoot and the stylist I hired for the first time, and now I am hooked! I decided that since I was shedding the WEIGHT of the first 50 years of my life, GO BIG or GO HOME.

I have struggled with obesity most of my adult life, weighing 322 pounds in 2015. I was always big-boned, thick, as some would say, and the Slaughter women (my mom's side of the family) have curvy shapely bodies.

In November 2022, I started to shed more of the mental WEIGHT. I began to feel a shift, which started to impact me internally. That shift started to peel back layers and reveal talents I never knew existed, allowing me to launch my coaching business, "The Growth Motivator™." Low key, I've been motivating others for decades but never wanted to be a coach.

So let me introduce myself! My name is Dr. Lisa L. Campbell®, The Growth Motivator™, and I help individuals and organizations, Shed the Weight™," that's been holding them hostage. Simply put, I help others shed the WEIGHT they've been carrying to enjoy life as their best version. To be clear, I hold a Ph.D. in Health Care Administration, so I am not a personal trainer, social worker, psychologist, or psychiatrist. Still, I am a woman who spent decades carrying WEIGHT. Once I experienced a mindset shift, I made it my mission to help others.

During my process, the years carrying my WEIGHT, there were times when I lost my way, but I never lost sight of who I was. Did I have some bad days? Absolutely because I'm human and I'm not perfect, but those defining moments in my life continued to allow me to grow and persist into the grandmother, the mother, the woman, the wife, the sister, the daughter, the aunt, the friend, the mentor, the leader, the teacher, that I am today. I motivate those that I encounter and work with to be the best version of themselves, even when I am not trying. I have an infectious spirit.

For the next 50 years of my life, I have big plans. I will help others Shed the WEIGHT, whatever that WEIGHT may be.

My grandfather, Edward Sr., is currently 102. Sometimes we are consumed by what's happening around us, and we focus on other people's accomplishments: graduations, business growth, marriages, promotions, financial success, etc. Sometimes we wonder *when it will be our time*, but sometimes, it's not our time because we carry too much WEIGHT. You don't have the capacity for your heart's desires yet.

Keep reading because you're going to walk away not only learning about what I endured during my 50 years of the WEIGHT I was carrying and got rid of, but together we will stop and allow time for reflection. If you don't have a copy of the journal accompanying this book, I recommend purchasing it today! As you are shedding the weight, you must write it down to memorialize the moments in real-time.

What will it take for you to go to the next level that will make you happier and more self-aware of who you are? I am living proof that when you take that WEIGHT and put it in the trash, you will see improvement in your relationships, friendships, employment situations, or how you approach work and many other instances.

Further, you will re-think those toxic relationships. So, listen, my dear readers, imagine we are back in the '80s, and it's clean-up week. It's time to clean out all the clutter and excess WEIGHT. You can see the path that's ahead of you!

CHAPTER ONE
Life Challenges

Standing in front of the mirror staring at myself in my bedroom a few months before I turned fifty, I started thinking about how my life changed.

On March 1, 1992, at the young age of eighteen, just thirty days before my nineteenth birthday, I gave birth to my one and only biological daughter Jasmine who was born in Blue Island, Illinois. A suburb south of Chicago where gardening took place every season. Beautiful landscapes of manicured lawns, purple crocuses, and yellow daffodils were sprouting too soon before spring because a wave of warm weather came for a few days but now it is cold again.

At thirty-four weeks pregnant my labor had to be induced because I lost fluid from around the placenta. The doctor brought me in to induce my labor. My Mother Yolanda, my rock, was there with me every step of the way, and after several hours of inducement, my OB-GYN told my mother to go home and that they would call her when it would be time to return. The induction failed and so I was taken to the operating room for an emergency C-Section. An attempt was made to do an epidural, but it failed and general anesthesia was given.

Jasmine was born at 6:27 AM and weighed 4 pounds 14 ounces. After the operation, I was surrounded by a support system that consisted of my mother and my aunt Lynette, who is also my Godmother. About three hours after having my C-Section, I will never forget my Auntie Lynette said, "Get up, time to get out of this bed and start walking."

You see, I come from a foundation of extremely strong women. My grandmother Ruby Slaughter set the bar high and we all in some shape, form, or fashion carry characteristics of her with us as we navigate life. Miss Ruby said what she meant and meant what she said. She enjoyed life to the fullest. Having no regrets!

Now back to Lynette, a Registered Nurse, and the family drill sergeant and advocate when it comes to healthcare. "You can't lie in this bed. You've got to get up. You got to walk around because you are going to be taking your baby girl home and she needs you. The longer you stay in bed, the harder it is to heal." So, we walked!

Jasmine and I stayed in the hospital for seven days. She would only eat if I breastfed her, and so I did. I had no plans to breastfeed. I just assumed that she would have a bottle. This is when my Jasmine journey began! We quickly learned that Jasmine could not drink regular baby formula and so via the Women, Infants and Children's (WIC) formula program, we were able to obtain Soy formula.

The nurse came into my room while my mom and aunt sat beside my bed and said that the pediatrician would be by shortly to share something with me. We could not wait to hear what the doctor had to say. I became anxious, and it started showing.

Mom says, "We should just wait to see what the doctor has to say."

"Yes, we do not need to think of anything wrong until we hear from the doctor," Aunt Lynette replied.

Tears started rolling down my face, and I was filled with emotional distress. This was not going to help me get better.

"Don't worry. You have not gotten any news," Mom encouraged.

Aunt Lynette stood up and held my hand patting it with her other hand.

"Everything is going to be fine. Just wait and see."

I felt something inside of me that was not right. There was an uneasy feeling deep down. A mother knows when something is wrong with her child.

The pediatrician finally came to see me after making his rounds with other patients. He walked over to my bed and said, "Jasmine is doing well but we had to do a CT scan and it identified that she has experienced some bleeding in her brain." Seven days later, when we were discharged, follow-up testing showed that the bleeding has disappeared.

At the time, I lived with my mother, and let me tell you if it wasn't for my mom, I would not have ever survived the first three months of motherhood. I read the book "What to Expect When You're Expecting," but in my opinion, having a baby is not like learning how to drive a car! In no way did it prepare me for the journey that I was about to embark on. Motherhood is full of uncertainty, and you will have to rely on your gut to make decisions. Don't get me wrong, the book was definitively informative, but the WEIGHT that I was about to endure was completely more than I could have ever imagined.

Jasmine, you see, liked to wake up every four hours for a feeding. As a person who likes eight to nine hours of sleep every night, Jasmine was interrupting my flow. So, Grandma Yolanda got up and made sure Jasmine was fed. This was 1992 and till this day, Jasmine does not require much sleep and still loves to eat.

1993

Twelve months after Jasmine was born, Mom said, "It is time for you to move out on your own." This is where adulting began and some mild depression started rearing its ugly head. Reluctantly, with minimal income, I got my first apartment in the basement of a friend's mother's home. This was not the best place to live as it was a concrete basement, but it was the best I could do at the time.

During this time, as I was living on my own, Mom informed me that Jasmine was not progressing like a baby should. My mom had two biological children, and she knew what to look for in how a baby should be developing. I scheduled an appointment for Jasmine to see the neighborhood doctor, Dr. Pedro. I'll never forget that name because he was also the doctor that everybody took their children to in our community. In fact, my father, uncles, and aunts had also seen him as children. After examining Jasmine, Dr. Pedro said, "Well not all kids progress at the same rate."

I went to my mom to share the good news with her about how Jasmine is progressing. A few weeks later, Mom said, "Something is wrong with Jasmine. She is rolling over, but you know, by now one year of age, she should be walking or attempting to walk."

1994

For 12 months, I lived in Clarksdale, Mississippi, and attended school in a single-parent dorm. During this time, Jasmine went to the doctor once and I did spend time worrying about how she was progressing, but after returning home, I realized that I needed to figure out what was wrong as she was about to turn three and still wasn't walking.

1995

After conducting some research, I made an appointment at La Rabida Children's Hospital in Chicago in the Jackson (Andrew) Park area. The hospital had a multi-specialty clinic which consisted of clinicians from different specialties and therapists to assist with the diagnoses of children. I will never forget Jasmine's developmental pediatrician's name, Dr. Thomas Blondis. He treated me with the upmost respect and his bedside manners were excellent. He was also quite the record keeper, didn't trust computers, but ensure that he maintained paper copies of all encounters. Dr. Blondis ordered diagnostic tests which included blood, hearing, occupational, speech, and physical therapy evaluations.

The first diagnosis was that Jasmine was born with cytomegalovirus (CMV). This virus was transmitted through the birth canal. Given that I only had sex with one person, I am pretty sure how this infection was obtained. According to the Mayo Clinic, most babies who have congenital CMV appear healthy at birth. However, some babies who have congenital CMV develop signs over time, sometimes not for months or years after birth. The most common of these late-occurring signs are hearing loss and developmental delay.

Jasmine was sent for a hearing test called an Auditory Brain Response (ABR) and the results showed that Jasmine has profound to severe sensorineural hearing loss in both ears. Unfortunately, we figured that something was wrong with her hearing because Jasmine didn't respond when we called her name. Effective December 31, 2002, in Illinois, a hearing test must be conducted at birth, but back then they did not test for hearing.

Also, at this time, Jasmine was not walking so the physical therapist conducted an evaluation and determined that Jasmine would benefit from Ankle Foot Orthotic (AFO). The purpose of the AFO is to improve stability so that Jasmine can safely walk when she was ready.

At this point, Jasmine was three years old and being fed with a bottle with a big hole in the nipple. The team at LaRabida recommended that we enroll Jasmine in an early intervention program for children who are developmentally delayed.

We decided to enroll her in Blue Cap which at the time was a program for developmentally delayed children in Blue Island, Illinois. They had an early intervention program in place for children who were three to five years old.

During the enrollment process at Blue Cap, Jasmine was given an Individualized Education Plan (IEP), which created a program for her to receive speech, occupational, and physical therapy services three times per week. The IEP process was very intimidating, but after a while, I realized that this planning process was important to establish goals to help her grow and develop. It was also my first exposure to SMART goals. We will explore the meaning later as I am going to challenge you to create some of your own. It also included social support services for us both as by this time, I was falling apart. As her mother, I was her advocate and her voice, so that others would know what her needs would be. This was a difficult time because I was having a hard time finding my voice.

In Jasmine's younger years, despite her disabilities, she was always happy and could often be heard laughing for no apparent reason. It was almost like God was speaking to her. We never knew what she was thinking or how she was feeling. Because Jasmine could not hear, she was not speaking.

In the early intervention program, they recommended that I take sign language, so I enrolled at the South Suburban Recreational Association (SSRA). One of my younger sisters Misty, who is four years younger than me attended the class with me and she was able to catch on to the signs much faster than I could. At the same time, Jasmine was being taught sign language, but ultimately, Jasmine made her own sign language to communicate to us what she needed. Even today, Jasmine will point to what she wants, she will pull you to what she needs, and you better get it taken care of because Jasmine is not one to wait for anything or anyone!

Jasmine's father chose not to be in her life. He said, "I don't know how to care for a child with special needs." News flash, neither do I. Life became difficult in Chicago. It was rough. I did whatever it took like any other mother would do. I figured it out.

1997

Once I completed my bachelor's degree, I struggled to care for Jasmine as she continued to experience developmental delays. A Caucasian woman at Blue Cap suggested that I put Jasmine in a residential facility. She said, "Jasmine will get care at the facility, she will grow." I presented the idea to a couple of people that were close to me. They both agreed that Black people don't put their loved ones in a home and then asked if I was crazy. I was confused and hurt all at the same time. But then I decided to trust my inner voice, same voice I heard, the day I decided against terminating my pregnancy. God will take care of her; I knew he had his hand of protection on her.

I struggled with this idea because I did not have the skills to care for Jasmine at home any longer, so I made the decision that was best for both Jasmine and me. The name of the facility is Phillip Rock in Glen Ellyn, Illinois. When I dropped Jasmine off, I'll never forget, the evening supervisor, Minister Wanda. She was the one who managed the program. At this time, Jasmine still wasn't walking. She was five years old. Wanda said, "Jasmine is going to be all right. We're going to take good care of her, Mom."

I knew that I had to do this for Jasmine because I could not care for her in the way that she deserved. I had to do what was best for her. While all these thoughts were swarming in my mind, the guy I was dating at the time had to literally pick me up and carry me out because, at that moment, I did not want to leave her. I just couldn't, but somehow, I got the inner strength that rose in me to do what was best. This inner strength in me came from my mother. She is a gentle soul, but as I said earlier, she comes from a strong-willed woman, my maternal grandmother Ruby Slaughter.

2006

I was instructed to enroll Jasmine in the Hope Center located in Springfield, Illinois. Phillip Rock advised that the Hope Center could care for her better, so I transferred her. As you know, I lived in the south suburbs of Chicago. It was rough because Jasmine's behavior increased during this time. She was more expressive.

When you have a child with special needs, the number of resources that are available for mental health, in general, is limited. As an African American mother, I saw first-hand how resources were not as available as information is to other ethnic people.

When I applied for Social Security Disability for Jasmine, it took nine months for us to get approved. Then months later I was sent a redetermination letter that indicated that Jasmine was not eligible because I made too much money. I was trying to figure out who determines these metrics.

The money I made covered rent, my car note, and for me to get back and forth to work, including whatever the state would not cover for Jasmine. Every expense was on me. I even applied for a Section 8 Voucher and was never contacted.

When you must take care of special needs children, there is a lack of available resources. Every time there is a cut in the budget at governmental agencies that is a place that receives limited care. It is never advertised what is available. Minority parents that have special needs children oftentimes do not know what resources are available and oftentimes don't know what questions to ask.

It crossed my mind what my mom said, *children don't ask to come here*. I did what I had to do and that was to make sure that Jasmine was fine. Everything I do is about the care that Jasmine will require once I am no longer on this earth.

I also did not receive child support or any support from Jasmine's father. My mother continued to encourage me that Jasmine was going to be taken care of and that she would never want for anything. I am so grateful. I'm so grateful for the people that God has placed in my life. I'm so grateful for the strength that he has given me to persevere no matter what.

Later, I will share with you my spiritual journey, which was built on a solid foundation. But, like any other journey has had its ups on downs! In the second part of my spiritual journey, while attending my second church home, St. James Ministries, my Pastor's wife preached a sermon with the title of, you must trust God, even when you can't trace him!

As a child, I was not good at art. I would get sketch paper and trace the lines of drawings that were already on another sheet of paper. I was good at science but not art. I thought about this in comparison with not being able to trace God and finding that he can be traced by looking at what he has already done for Jasmine and me. This reminder built my faith even more because at first, I could not see it until she reminded me.

Meanwhile at the Hope Center, which was far from where I lived. Driving there and back home took three hours there and three hours back, which meant most of our visits were spent in the car! Because of the distance, I could not see her as much as I would have liked. Having a special needs child that could not talk scared me. I would always wonder if someone was harming her. Harm is not always visible, which is scary. FaceTime wasn't an option back then!

2008

My best friend Adriane, Paul (who is now my husband) and I went and moved Jasmine from the Hope Center in Springfield, Illinois. The facility had to double clients in one room. Because Jasmine doesn't like to have a roommate, she reacted to having someone else in the room. Jasmine loves her own personal space. She does not like to share a room with anybody. Paul and I were dating at the time, and he cared so much about what Jasmine was going through and how it affected me. Now, Paul reminds me regularly, he should have been Jasmine's father, but after we reconnected, he took on the title of Dad.

She is my only biological child. I have three bonus children, Paul, Jr., Raven, and Tiffany. Both blended families are a package deal. We cannot accept one without the other. All three love Jasmine as if she was their blood sister. They understand her special needs.

Also, in 2008, Jasmine went to her third residential facility, Little City Foundation in Palatine, Illinois. While Jasmine was there, she got to go to her prom. They had a prom every year. Life was great for her. She continued growing and developing into a young lady. This facility has all kinds of programs and activities in place that parents looked forward to attending.

One year, Zhane, Jasmine's big little sister, who is a professional makeup artist, did Jasmine's makeup. When I first met Zhane (who is two years younger than Jasmine) and her mother Hosanna at Chicago State University in 1996, she would push Jasmine in her stroller when they both were younger. Zhane is my unofficial second-oldest daughter. She was Jasmine's protector!

Jasmine hated going to the store back then, but she needed a prom dress. Grandma Yolanda loved shopping for her. She went and bought 10 dresses every year from stores at Lincoln Mall which was in Matteson, Illinois, which is no longer in existence – a place where my grandmother, Miss Ruby, loved to frequent.

We put our heads together to decide which one looked perfect for Jasmine. She really enjoyed getting dressed up and then experiencing fun at her prom. Little City Foundation made a great impression on Jasmine, although, there were experiences where Jasmine felt uncomfortable. This is to be expected at any facility.

Each facility that she was a resident of assisted Jasmine in her development. Each stage of her development was critical to her wellbeing. I knew some cared about her, especially at Phillip Rock. She had to leave, there were staff who had her best interest at heart. Although there were three ladies, who I knew loved Jasmine as if she was their child: Joyce, Janice, and Anissa, who I keep in touch with today. The point I am making here is they would braid Jasmine's hair making sure she looked good, kept her clean, and made sure she felt great. You see when you have an African American child, hair is a big thing.

What I was not able to do for my daughter, I was able to do with my other children who are my bonus children. When you have a child(ren) that does not have any disabilities, it still takes a lot of work assisting them in their development. It can be tough. I had the privilege of being extremely influential to my bonus children. I taught them how to drive, took them on college tours, was able to experience seeing them off to their prom, and we have gone on vacations.

2013

Jasmine was nearing the age where she was no longer eligible to receive services at Little City Foundation because of her age. My mother, hubby Paul, paternal Auntie Phyllis, and I went to visit several adult facilities. There are day program facilities and then there are Community Integrated Living Arrangements (CILA's), which is usually the place where you live. We all went to visit one place after another.

Some facilities had concrete floors where clients went during the day. At this point in time, Jasmine spent most of her time on the floor and other times she spent in her rocking chair. She loves her rocking chair and rolling around on the floor. Both are her happy places. So, any place with concrete floors was not suitable for her. And so, we looked, and we looked, and we looked.

In Jasmine's records, there was some information about behavioral problems, which made finding an adult facility that would accept her a challenge. On paper, she did appear to be a resident that would fit well into most facilities. It became exhausting, so I got to a point where I said, "Hubby, let's buy a house and open up our own community-integrated living arrangement (CILA)." I said this because we could get a CILA that Jasmine could live in, and other people could too. For instance, a four-bedroom house.

All three of us, Auntie Phyllis, Paul, and I went to Springfield, Illinois to attend a class on the requirements to open a facility. There were of course financial obligations and other things needed to start and run a facility. One must be prepared to provide support 24 hours a day, 365 days a year and this means we would be 100% responsible for the entire operation.

Additionally, I became very disturbed while attending the class. There were people there only wanting to know when they would be getting paid. Oh, that sent me through more emotional challenges. This was for my baby, Jasmine. So, we kept looking to find her somewhere suitable for her condition. I ultimately realized that while opening a CILA sounded like a great idea, being responsible for others' loved ones was not a risk I was willing to assume.

One day we went to Sequin, a place that did not have concrete floors in their day program area. The house where Jasmine would be staying looked like a house that was made specifically for her.

I am Jasmine's voice, and if she never utters a word, as long as I live, I must be her voice that speaks for her. She has her way of communicating and expressing herself. I wish parents would understand the power they have and be the voice that their children need because maybe the world would not be like it is today.

We decided to go with Sequin. Jasmine has been there for 10 years now. They tried putting her in a room with someone else, but she didn't want a roommate. She has been living an amazing life. One that she is comfortable with.

Believe it or not, Jasmine has been on a cruise. Let me tell you, Grandma Yolanda, Paul, and I were sitting on pins and needles wondering how she was going to respond to a different surrounding. The cruise life, while it is my favorite, it did not agree with Jasmine, the buffet wasn't open when she wanted to eat, and Jasmine didn't like the fact that we had to wait to board the ship. It was this trip that we discovered how fast Jasmine could slip away as she broke away from Auntie Linda's tight hand grip and attempted to board the ship in a matter of seconds.

Jasmine got on the plane and went to Disney World. Yes, she went to Magic Kingdom and all the different places in Disney World that you can enjoy. When she was younger, she loved to swim, floating on her back. To watch her float was to experience peace.

One thing I was concerned about, and am wondering is, what was Jasmine thinking. She seems at peace and knows how to express herself when she needs something. I was still concerned about what was on her mind. It seems like she does not have a clue about what's going on in the world. I know that she doesn't know that we were in a pandemic. She doesn't know that we have four different seasons. Now, I will tell you this, the girl loves her *some sun*, so maybe in that respect, she does know about the different seasons.

God gave Jasmine to me because he knew that I could handle it. Even if I did not always understand or know because it was all new to me, God knew. He gave me the strength and the foundation that I needed to successfully navigate my growth journey.

You too will have to find within yourself the strength deep down on the inside to look at situations and use them as stepping stones.

My "Shed the Weight™" Moments:

1. You can't make an impact if you continue to lie down and don't take the first step.
2. Trust your gut, if something keeps tugging at you internally, you owe it to yourself to investigate it further.
3. You must learn to advocate for the most important person, you!!!
4. Just because someone doesn't look like you don't mean you should devalue their expertise and recommendations.
5. Life does not sit still; growth requires development in or to allow progression to occur.
6. Your voice is your communication tool, don't take it for granted, some people aren't born with theirs.

Open your "GROW With Me™" journal and follow the prompts provided.

Chapter Two
The Education Journey

Growing up with parents who worked jobs without a college education, I never really considered college. My father worked at the Post Office and my mother for an insurance company in a clerical role.

1993

Exactly two years post-graduation from high school, I took the ACT exam which is designed to predict your ability to be admitted to college and to some extent, illustrates how successful you will be in college. Well, at the time, I never really had any plans to attend a university. The real reason that I took the ACT was because I decided to attend Coahoma Community College in Clarksdale, Mississippi because they had a Single Parent Program. The ACT was one of the requirements for admission and so I took the exam.

This exam consisted of four parts: English, math, reading and science. In my earlier years, I was not a great test taker, and I was a nervous wreck waiting on those results. After a few weeks they arrived. On the ACT score report, you are provided with a composite score, which is your total number of correct answers converted to a score that ranges from one to 36, which is based on an average of the four tests.

My ACT composite score was 17. According to the score report, which, yes, I still have today, my composite score suggests that I would only be eligible for college admissions with a focus on liberal arts. This policy is open to everyone, so that means I wasn't in the category of being a highly sought after student. It's funny because today, I am a highly sought after speaker, who loves to read and write!

You may be wondering how I became Dr. Lisa L. Campbell®. How did you ever earn a doctorate degree? How did you get a master's degree? For that matter, how did you even finish college? Well, one of the things that I've learned is that an ACT score and an IQ score can predict how successful one will be in school. A high level of emotional intelligence can determine how successful one is going to be in life. So, you see, while I quote and unquote wasn't destined for college success, I've always been destined for greatness.

I scored a 14 in reading and math, and I don't like math, but I scored a 19 in English and science, so this probably makes sense. Why? I'm in healthcare today. Was that 17 composite score, the cream of the crop when it comes to college admissions? Absolutely not. But having a growth mindset allowed me to persevere during my educational journey.

What's interesting is that 30 years later, I learned that while ACT scores are said to determine success in college, it was my level of emotional intelligence that helped me grow by leaps and bounds. Further, my trials and tribulations gave me a *can't stop, won't stop* mentality. As Uncle Asa III would often say, I'm a Slaughter, and always do what I must do! Let me take you back to my first encounter in school where my journey as an authentic unstoppable leader began.

In 1978, I was a kindergartner at Wendell Smith Elementary School, located at 744 East 103rd Street in Chicago. My mother, father, one-year-old sister, and I lived in an apartment right off East 103rd Street.

As a kindergartner, I went to school for a half-day. Because my mother worked during the day, my father, who worked evenings, was responsible for picking me up. Now, my father generally is a punctual individual. On this day I waited, and after what seemed like an eternity, as a self-motivated five-year-old leader, I had a decision to make. Since I didn't have a cell phone and don't even remember if I knew my home phone number to call my father to pick me up, and wanted to watch Sesame Street, I put a plan in place. I was aware of the route I needed to take to go home, and I wasn't afraid to take that first step.

Back in those days, communities were safer than they are now. I was at a crossroad. What do I do? Do I go back inside the school and allow one of the officials to contact my father or my mother and let them know that I wasn't picked up or do I walk home by myself? Even at that age, I made an executive decision to walk home.

Wendell Smith Elementary School was about three to four blocks from my home, 535 E. 102nd Street. I said to myself, just *walk the same way that daddy drives you to school and you'll be home in no time*. So, I did. When I got home, I rang the doorbell. My father, who again worked evenings, had overslept. He was surprised that I came home by myself. Shortly thereafter, he purchased me a T-shirt that says, *One Day I'll Be President* and he was right. I am president of three individual companies. Wow!

1982

This was the year that my parents had gotten a divorce. Now I know that divorce can have an enormous impact on children. The day that my parents told us, my sister and I, I will never forget we were in the bathtub. One of my parents said, "We are getting a divorce."

Now, I don't know if we received the infamous statements, you know the one that says, "This has nothing to do with you. This is all about us and our love for one another." My sister and I both had different reactions. In fact, I recall having no reaction at all. I saw the signs, I heard the arguments, so my inner logical self knew something was going on and this was the conclusion of that something. That was my reaction. That's how I dealt with the news. Now, I will tell you as a child, at the age that I was, I wasn't naïve. I knew something was going on, and that one day my sister and I would move from 738 West 119th Street to 1404 West 119th Street.

1983

Now, this was at the time I was in the fourth and fifth grade attending West Pullman, which was not too far from where my father lived. Prior to that, I had attended a school called

Whistler Elementary for first, second and third grade. That was down the street from where my grandparents lived on Loomis Avenue in Chicago. Moving not too far from my grandparents was amazing. My grandparents were such loving grandparents. I can remember, my aunts and uncles would always say, *you got a different version of granddad than what we got*. Well, as a new grandmother myself, I could see the difference between being a parent versus a grandparent.

My parents divorced when I was in third grade. The elementary school I attended for fourth and fifth grade was near my father's house. So, my parents decided it would be best if we switched schools so that they could figure out their new normal, operating as co-parents living apart.

I am the first born of my mother's two children and have always been a leader. Prior to leaving Whistler Elementary School to attend the school by my dad's house, the teacher told my mom that I was reading at a first-grade level and would have to repeat the third grade because my standardized test scores demonstrated that I was not ready to be in fourth grade. Going into fourth grade while reading at a first-grade level would be challenging. I've always wondered about the validity of standardized tests. I don't recall learning the art of test, testing nor do I recall being prepared for the test.

You may be wondering how I remember all of this, it's because I have a photographic memory! For a long time, I thought I wasn't smart enough. I always exemplified leadership qualities. So, when I went to the new school at West Pullman, the proctor said the test was not accurate. I was able to start in fourth grade. This is where I met Jasmine's father. But I didn't see him again until my senior year in high school.

Our relationship was a typical high school relationship! We met, he had a car and would pick me up from McDonald's, which is where I worked as a manager and of course would get free food. Shortly thereafter, Jasmine was born, I quickly realized that parenthood would be a journey that I would experience without him. Thankfully, his mother always did and does continue to keep in touch with us.

1984

I told my mom that I missed my friends, so I went back to Whistler for six, seventh, and eighth grade. Whistler was an exciting time for me as I was growing with my childhood friends from the neighborhood. I met one of my very close friends Genita in eighth grade when she transferred to our school from Los Angeles. She used to come over to the house and wrap my hair. That was when the wrap hairstyle first came out. The style was to wrap your hair like a beehive and place a silk scarf around it to keep hair neat while you sleep and then unwrap it when you awaken.

I pretty much stayed in the house during my sixth, seventh, and eighth grade years. I was raised in the era that you were home when the streetlights came on. The exciting part is that I was graduating. I had an opportunity to sing at my eighth-grade graduation. Now, don't be confused. I am a background singer. I am not a lead singer, but music and singing became my community for most of my adult life.

As an eighth grader, you do what you are asked to do, so I did. Of course, I've never shied away from the microphone. In fact, today, most days I fall asleep having just left a microphone. It's my happy place. It's where I can speak to thousands of people and have an impact.

After graduation, I went to Fenger High School. I did not want to go to Fenger. Why? Because most of my classmates from Whistler Elementary went to Fenger. Coincidentally, my father, uncles and aunts also attended Fenger when they were younger. This was the neighborhood high school. I had hopes of attending Morgan Park High School, which is the high school that my mom attended. We did not live in the district, but my Grandmother Ruby did.

I asked my mom if I could use Grandma Ruby's address, so I could attend Morgan Park. Mom, a woman of integrity said, "No. You're going to Fenger." Oh! I hated her response, but I did what I was told. In my first year of high school, I met my now husband, Paul.

1987

I had the typical high school experience. I met new friends – not a lot and was in the choir as a background singer. Because I was and have always been shapely, I joined the Modeling Club. My hips was what I loved about my girlish figure. I had enrolled in the Principal Scholars' Program which allowed me to take advanced classes. Back then, I never thought I was smart. Nor was I acknowledged for being one of the students headed for college.

1989

Now, the moment I turned sixteen, I started working at McDonald's and really focused on getting out of high school so that I could work and have my own money. We did not have a money tree in our backyard, because growing up in a single parent household, money was scarce. This was during the same time I connected with Jasmine's father. He was my prom date in my senior year.

At the same time, I was working at McDonald's as a manager, at a young age. I had attended Hamburger University and thought that I would one day own a McDonald's. I started as a cashier, making $3.35 per hour, and by 1992 I was making $5.90 per hour. I loved being able to make my own money, which in turn helped my mom who was a single parent for most of my childhood. Additionally, I was able to buy myself whatever I wanted, which was the start of my lifelong process of having multiple streams of income.

1991

Prom time was finally here, and I was so excited. I am grateful that I was able to continue working because I was to pay majority of my prom expenses. At a very young age, I was responsible and enjoyed working. I attribute that to my Aunt Phyllis, who let me work for her while in elementary school.

I can recall creating deposit slips for her business account making deposits as well as paying bills for her. She also allowed me to iron her clothes to earn money. I ironed her outfits that she wore to the skating rink. Phyllis loved skating! In fact, she would skate seven days per week. She also worked a part time job. As I had gotten older, I realized that many facets of who I am today stem from parts of her. Of course, much more refined and organized, chuckle! I will share more about Aunt Phyllis in another chapter.

I enjoyed working at McDonald's because I had an opportunity to learn about managing people, processes, and resources. As a manager, I was responsible for counting money and products. At the end of my shift, it included but was not limited to identifying what was sold and what was wasted. Thankfully, my Auntie Phyllis's training had prepared me for management. I've learned that you should not leave any experiences behind. They are part of who you are and what you have to offer to the world in any situation. Don't you ever let anyone discount your experience, it belongs to you, and they can't take it away.

1992

Shortly after giving birth, I realized that my dream of owning a McDonald's had to be put on hold because the cost of baby formula and diapers were an expense that I didn't expect to be so costly. One day while sitting at home watching television, this was before social media, I saw a commercial for a Medical Assistant Program. In just six short months I could have a career in healthcare.

My Auntie Lynette wanted me to become a nurse. I didn't really want to become a nurse. I watched her transition from a Licensed Practical Nurse (LPN) to a Registered Nurse (RN). I eventually thought, *what is good for her is good for me.*

I went to school at the National Education Center-Bryman Campus in Oak Lawn, Illinois to become a Medical Assistant (MA) with a goal of working in a physician's office. The program was very fast paced, and it was set up as a rolling modular program, which meant, when I began the program, I intermingled with students that were about to graduate.

I will never forget how intense that first class was because in this module, we had to give each other injections. Here I was a new mom and was injecting saline water into other students with little knowledge of medical terminology and human anatomy. Just like anything else I had experienced at the time, I embraced the challenge and met a few friends. Tara, one of the friends I met, who was slightly older than me (inside joke) and together we successfully completed that module.

1993

One of my former McDonald's co-workers and friend Sheila said, "There is a single parent dorm in Clarksdale, Mississippi at Coahoma Community College. We should go." Sheila, who had a little boy, one year younger than Jasmine, felt that we could help each other out. She had conducted extensive research and learned that they had recently created a single parent dorm.

After attending school for medical assisting, I felt now was my opportunity to become a nurse. One thing about me, I will try most anything once. I come from a very spiritual family, but I will tell you during that time, I lost my way. I'll never forget, I went to my Aunt Phyllis who is everybody's favorite aunt. She gave me some money and said, "Good luck."

GROW WITH ME

There was no one to take me to Mississippi, so Jasmine and I took the Greyhound bus which was fifteen hours one way to Clarksdale, Mississippi. When I think back on this, I ask myself, what were you thinking! I now know I was growing! My mindset was growth!

Sheila's family was excited about her journey and her parents drove her to Mississippi. I don't recall if my parents couldn't or wouldn't take us, but I believe my trials and tribulations during that year made me who I am today. Some journeys require you to walk alone! If you don't have experiences, you cannot grow! Growth is a vibe! Growth is powerful!

What attracted me to this college was it had a daycare. They accepted Jasmine, who was not walking and confined her to a stroller. During this time, Jasmine was very young and didn't really require a lot of support as she was still presenting as a baby.

About a week after we arrived, Jasmine was exposed to chicken pox. We had to go home. Jasmine and I traveled another 15 hours by bus. She screamed and hollered on the bus the entire time. I was helpless and alone. I kept telling God, "If you could just let me make it home, I'll be all right." We finally made it home and about a week later, the chicken pox sores cleared up and we went back to Mississippi. Yes, back on the Greyhound we went.

Sheila and I stayed in a two-story dorm building which was managed by the dorm father who was the offensive football coach. Our dorm father, Coach Mitchell was the coolest person I met at the school. Shortly after my arrival, I was low on money, and he got me a work-study job as the Residence Assistant (RA). I also was able to get public assistance for food stamps, which was much less than I would have gotten in Chicago, but we survived.

The other mothers in the dorm instantly became my family! We were all on the same path, which was focused on making a better life for our children as single parents. While I don't recall all the ladies, I do remember Gwen, who I follow on Facebook, is married and is doing very well. Another mother, Edna was our choir leader/director for the school's gospel choir, which I joined immediately upon my arrival. Growing up attending church weekly, I needed to continue my spiritual journey.

During our first semester, there was no one on the second floor, but the second semester Coach Mitchell's offensive linemen all moved in and stayed on the second floor. Let's just say, we couldn't date anyone on the basketball team, even though Sheila married one of the basketball players. Otherwise, what happened in Clarksdale stays there!

Our dorm father pretty much let us do what we wanted to do! It was more like he was a big brother as opposed to a father. He was a nice-looking gentleman and was always very easy to talk to.

Jasmine and I spent two semesters at Coahoma with intentions of completing prerequisites to become a nurse, but I partied more than anything else.

After two semesters, my grades looked like this:

Subject	Grade
Zoology Lecture	D
Zoology Lab	F
Orientation	B
English	F
Gym	C
Sociology	C
Psychology	C
Chemistry Lecture	D
Chemistry Lab	F

1994

Returning home from Coahoma, I found myself at an impasse, so I enrolled at Robert Morris College, for medical assisting. This process was humbling because I had to start over, but luckily that photographic memory helped me excel. While the structure of this program was different, I knew pretty much everything that was being covered in that program. I can recall helping several students learn how to use the Medical Manager software. I love working on computers and I was in my zone! This is the same year I met my best friend Adriane, who also became Jasmine's godmother and my sister from another mother.

1995

One month before graduation, my advisor asked if I wanted to complete an associate degree program, majoring in Allied Health. I was on a mission; growth was on my mind! I had an opportunity to participate on the debate team, my team won first place! This year I really found my voice, I started creating power point slide decks and delivering stellar presentations.

I was in my Zone of Genius sharing the knowledge I had gained by researching new topics. I started feeling more focused. I felt my head was thinking clearer. However, there were times I had experienced periods of depression because I felt alone in my growth journey. I was traveling by public transportation; my days and nights were long. At the end of this year, I decided I needed a car.

1996

Once again, I graduated, this time I was smiling from inside out. This same year, RMC was starting a new bachelor's degree, with an emphasis in Healthcare Management. Quite naturally I decided that I was all in! By this time, I was working two jobs!

No one that I knew had a child with special needs. I didn't have anyone to share my deepest pain with! Honestly, at that point, I still didn't understand the extent of her disabilities.

I was young and still wanted to party. Ladies' night at the Clique nightclub in Chicago was one of my favorite places to hang out! I could be seen there doing the percolator, which is still my favorite song today.

Although, I come from a strong loving family, one day, the pressure was building up in my mind, so I decided to end my life by taking a bottle of pills. I told myself that I did not want to live. It was too much for me. I did not quite understand the decision I had made that forced me to grow up overnight. I don't know if I was looking for love that drove me to a state of depression or my responsibilities.

There were several events that transpired during that time and like any typical young person, I wanted to make sure I was there. It really made me even more depressed because I had to face my responsibilities as a mother and not attend. I am still here to share my story.

1997

I graduated from Robert Morris again with a bachelor's degree of Business Administration majoring in healthcare administration. After this experience, I decided that no one was ever going to define me by an ACT score, being a woman, or being a single parent. I would never allow those labels to impact my life.

After completing my bachelor's degree at Robert Morris, immediately, we moved from Blue Island, Illinois to Richton Park, Illinois so that I could be closer to Governors State University (GSU), which is where I enrolled to earn my master's degree. Richton Park was one town over from GSU.

This was the point in my life, where I realized it was time to hang up my Medical Assistant hat, so I applied for and got a full-time job teaching, medical office assisting. Not only was I teaching the entire program, but I also had to create all the course content. Those presentation skills were being elevated!

1998

While enrolled at GSU for my master's degree in healthcare administration, it was there that I met a good friend who made my life at GSU enjoyable. I call her Nurse Debra. She would encourage me when I was down, and I would do the same for her. She is 16 years older than me, so I had to help her navigate using the computer, which I still do today!! I don't mind it at all.

I had originally enrolled at GSU to earn a master's in business administration, but that first semester, calculus quickly made me realize that healthcare was my life! So, I went back to my roots and switched my major to Health Administration. Keep in mind, all my experience was in healthcare and the other was a manager at McDonald's.

1999

While attending GSU, I started working as a practice assistant at a cardiovascular clinic in Calumet City, Illinois. I had applied for the practice manager job, but the person interviewing me said, "I know you have your bachelor's degree, and I see you have a strong medical assistant background, so I want to bring you in as the practice assistant."

The practice manager position was given to a man with a Master of Business Administration (MBA). He did not bring to the table what I brought to the table. By this time, the knowledge I had gained relates to the operational and clinical aspects of a physician's practice, which was second to none. I could perform and manage all aspects of the revenue cycle.

It was at that point that I knew I was destined for more. I had to continue the educational process to obtain as much as I could to develop expediently. I realized that I was born for this and had to do whatever it takes to reach my destiny. There is a saying, that God would not put more on you than you can bear, so I was up for the challenge. I knew that I did not want to stop at the juncture of being a practice assistant.

I knew how to manage employees and the processes of opening and closing, along with ordering inventory and keeping a facility in tip top shape. This is because of my background experience of working at McDonald's and attending Hamburger University.

What kept going through my mind was the T-shirt my father gave me that said, *One Day I Will Be President*. So, I knew that practice assistant was not going to do it for me! I applied for a job at Cook County Hospital as a division administrator of general medicine. I was hired as an external candidate, which was amazing.

It was at Cook County hospital that I met David Fagus (RIP), a brilliant data analyst, who was part of the interviewing process. One day during lunch, I asked him, "Why did you hire me?" I was not a current employee of the county system and had no health care management experience. He said, "Well, I figured if you could manage a McDonald's, you could manage people in this organization."

Day one at Cook County Hospital, I hit the ground running, with nothing more than a desk and a computer. To make matters worse, the budget was due in two weeks after I had started there. I had to manage staff who were union members. I was very young at the time and received a lot of grief from these employees.

2000

Nurse Debra and I graduated from GSU in May. Nurse Debra went off to continue her journey as a nurse, eventually working for the federal government. By now, you know me, there was always more!

In August, I applied at Moraine Valley Community College (MVCC) and enrolled in the coding specialist program. I had performed the medical coding function, but I really had not been officially trained in it, so I decided to go to school for it to really learn it from A to Z. I met a wonderful professional named Charlotte, who helped me realize the importance of coding guidelines as a critical component to the medical coding process. While at MVCC, I realized that experience is great, but formal training does have a role and should not be undervalued.

2001

May of this year, I completed the Coding Specialist certificate program at MVCC. I know you are probably thinking, what's next? I continued working hard at Cook County, but since I did not have any political affiliations, I was not able to obtain a higher position. What I thought to myself, *I cannot grow here*! After applying for three positions higher than mine, that I was more than qualified for according to the job description, I resigned! Yup, good benefits and a position, I left it behind.

2002

I started working at South Suburban Community College full time and there I was a coordinator of three programs, medical assisting, medical coding, and medical transcription.

One day, a physician, Dr. Matthew Johnson, called the campus asking if anyone could help him with his billing! As the coordinator, of course, the call was routed to me! I decided to go over to the office and for several days, I performed an operational assessment and workflow for all aspects of his billing process. The office has just purchased a billing system and now that the system was installed, the sales guy was nowhere to be found!

Using PowerPoint and drawing from my experience, I created a list of recommendations and Dr. Johnson asked me to implement them and train his staff, which consisted of a front desk clerk and a medical assistant.

It felt really good to be back in the physician's office. I didn't miss working as a MA. I realized that helping physicians and their practices was my calling! At the end of our time together, Dr. Johnson asked me to send him my invoice. As a 9:00-5:00 and generally a salaried professional, I was puzzled, but immediately said no problem. I went home and came up with what I thought was a fair fee. Two weeks later a check arrived at my home.

After that experience, I created my first company, Physician Practice Resources, Inc. to support the operational effectiveness of Physician Practices.

2004

After a while, I realized I needed to make more money, so I went to the Human Resources coordinator and asked, "How can I make more money?"

Her response was, "Get a second master's degree."

I searched the internet and found Capella University. When I contacted their administrative office, they were willing to accept a lot of credits that I had already received at GSU and since my master's was in healthcare administration and then my doctorate that I was pursuing was in healthcare administration, it worked out.

When I got to the doctoral program, I was chugging along, you know it, and I spaced. I felt alone a lot because I didn't have anyone in my family who could help me navigate through the doctoral journey. In fact, I didn't know anyone that had a doctorate degree. I was the first in my family to get a master's degree; the first in my family to get a doctorate degree. Shortly after enrolling, I convinced Nurse Debra to join me on the doctoral journey and she did!

2008

After going through the Institutional Review Board (IRB) and approval from my professional association, the American Health Information Management Association (AHIMA). I collected my data for my research study by conducting a 1:1 interview with those that graciously agreed to participate during our annual convention in Seattle, Washington. My now husband Paul and brother-in-law William joined me and helped me set up.

2009

Once the conference was over and I aggressively started evaluating my data. Finally, I was thinking, *yes, we're going to bring this to a close.* I had a setback. That setback was the Chair who was my Dissertation Chair had disappeared. I was left in limbo. I didn't have any guidance, so every term I was just enrolled. To make matters worse, I had scheduled and paid for a huge graduation party in Miami, where I spared no experience, from a memorable roof top party to a private charted yacht! Yes, this girl has always been on fire! Work hard, play harder is my motto!

Also, in 2009, I incorporated my business with the State of Illinois. The journey of entrepreneurship has been one of growth. My mission has always been to improve the operational effectiveness of those whom we serve.

2010

The student loan debt was piling up, the Financial Aid Department came to me and said, "You no longer have financial aid available to pay your tuition. You've *maxed* out on everything." When I tell you I was devastated, I was. I had to sit out. I was calling them trying to understand how this could happen. The financial aid advisor was giving me this song and dance, and I persistently called trying to get clarity as to why.

Why? When I think about my education journey, I think one of the things that I learned from the first program when the school closed. I learned to have a no matter what attitude. No matter what I was going to finish. Eventually, they discovered they made a mistake, and I was allowed to return to school.

I had been out for a while until the problem was solved, so the school allowed me to attend a writer's retreat. And that's where I was able to basically turn the corner with a new committee.

When Nurse Debra finished in 2008, it didn't really impact me. Because I was like, well, I'm collecting my data, so surely you know I'm right on her heels. I'll never forget, my pastor Bishop Willie James Campbell, may he rest in peace, said, "Never lose your confidence. You may have been delayed, but you will not be denied."

During that journey when I was told I couldn't return, I felt somewhat defeated. But I just kept holding on to the fact that if I just have faith the size of a mustard seed, I was going to be able to move this mountain, and I did.

2013

In March, I officially received my doctorate degree. Earlier, I had a huge three-day graduation party in 2009 in Miami South Beach, Florida. This became one of the driving forces for me to finish. You cannot have a party, walk across the stage, and not finish. Surely, I had to complete the journey that I started. If you haven't figured it out at this point, I believe in huge celebrations.

2015

Once the doctoral journey was officially over, I vowed to never ever, ever enroll in another program. Well, it turns out, I realized that I am a lifelong learner. I went back to school and received a second master's degree in project management. One of the things that I learned about myself is that I really enjoy projects. I enjoy seeing something through from start to finish by any means necessary.

When I am in the virtual or face to face classroom, educating the next generation of healthcare professionals, health information managers, and/or healthcare administrators, I'm tough on them. Because I am a witness and living proof that despite what may come your way, you can make it.

Now, I just didn't stop at academic training. I also hold eleven national certifications:

1. Certified Professional Coder (CPC),
2. Certified Outpatient Coder (COC),
3. Certified Professional Biller (CPB),
4. Certified Risk Coder (CRC),
5. Certified Professional Medical Auditor (CPMA),
6. Certified Coding Specialist-Physician Based (CCS-P),
7. Certified Coding Specialist (CCS),

8. Certified Documentation Improvement Practitioner (CDIP),
9. Certified Healthcare Compliance (CHC),
10. Registered Health Information Administrator (RHIA), and
11. AAPC Approved Instructor.

Because I never gave up, I continue to be a lifelong learner, I will excel.

In life, you too will have to face challenges in your educational journey, persevere during those most difficult times.

My "Shed the Weight™" Moments:

1. Do not let a test or exam define who you are.
2. The entirety of your being cannot be measured by a standardized test.
3. It's incredible how the individual who obtained a low score in reading is the same person who reads medical documents professionally and enjoys reading frequently.
4. From an early age, my mother demonstrated to me the significance of upholding integrity when making choices.
5. Having a few detours along the way does not imply that you won't reach your destination.
6. My journey in education taught me that results are achieved through patience, perseverance, commitment, hard work, and a positive mindset.

Open your "GROW With Me™" journal and follow the prompts provided.

CHAPTER THREE
Jasmine

In July 2022, a tragedy occurred to a five-year special needs boy in Richton Park, Illinois. A town that I lived in from 1998 to 2000 that really shook me to my core. A mother had enrolled her autistic son in a home-based daycare one that indicated that they could care for a special needs child. Apparently, in this situation, the father of the child had spoken with the caregiver on the same day that the incident happened. Not very long after dropping off his son, about thirty minutes later, the child had died. The caregiver had strapped him in a chair for thirty minutes so that they could take a shower. When I think about that situation, I immediately thought that could have been Jasmine.

I remember when I was younger, and I wanted to go out and party. I hired a babysitter from the newspaper and that's back in the day when babysitters would advertise in the newspaper. When I think back on that, I say to myself, *were you out of your mind? Was it that important for you to go to a party that you would entrust the care of your special needs daughter to a stranger.* Apparently, I was out of my mind or maybe I am just human. Raising a special needs child has really been an eye-opener. But also, the fact that I'm admitting this shows you my true authenticity as a person and a leader.

By profession, I am in healthcare and have worked in many clinical and non-clinical capacities. One of the areas focuses on managing health records, which coincidentally, I've kept records on Jasmine dating back to the day she was born. In fact, I have the bill and records from when she was born which makes it quite interesting.

The work I do today focuses on medical coding and clinical documentation integrity. I am vested in ensuring that health records are accurate and timely and can be used by internal and external stakeholders. This journey has been challenging in more than one way.

The first challenge was my emotions. As a young mother, a person who never wanted to have children, dealing with a special needs child was emotionally draining. Every night, I carry to bed with me the thought of someone harming her. If something did happened, will she be able to express it in her own way. What also keeps running through my mind is the autistic little boy who died. The thought of it keeps taking me back to when I was trying to find a babysitter for Jasmine.

I will never forget the number of people in different organizations that said, "Oh yes, we can care for special needs children." But honestly, I probably would have asked that question a little differently. Can you deal with an individual that is nonverbal? Do you have the patience to deal with someone who cannot articulate what their needs are – one that uses hand gestures to get what they need?

At thirty-one years old, Jasmine has no problem communicating her needs and everybody who cares for her knows what she is expressing when there is a need that isn't being met.

In the past, I had so many situations where caregivers would say they can deal with special needs children, and then at the end of the week, they stated, "It was a struggle. We cannot care for Jasmine."

Trying to work, go to school, and raise Jasmine would sometimes hurt deep in my soul. There were others who were close to me who couldn't help. I am thankful that my family members answered the call. At one point, I didn't have anywhere to live, and my Aunt Diane, without hesitation, let me move in with her for a few months. When I think back on that, I think about how blessed we are.

The second challenge was raising my daughter. There was one point, I went to my mom and said, "I cannot raise my daughter as a single parent." My mom told me, I will never forget, that Jasmine will never need for anything. I am so thankful that she hasn't had a need for anything that my community couldn't provide. We were never on the street, had to live in a homeless shelter, or didn't have to live in my car when I was younger. These were never an option for Jasmine and me. My family has always been there for us.

As I mentioned in a previous chapter, Jasmine has had the privilege to go to Disney World and on a cruise. While on the cruise, my husband and I felt somewhat stressed. Jasmine is deaf and has no fears. She loved to float in the pool and kept looking over in the ocean. It would be nothing for her to dive in, so we had to be sure that she did not. The great part is that she got a chance to experience being on a cruise.

Someone asked me if I did it for Jasmine or for myself. Honestly, it was for both of us. Well, let me say this, it's a privilege being Jasmine's mother and her protector, and Jasmine's legal guardian until I die, it was for both of us.

I don't know all the time what Jasmine is thinking, what she likes, what she doesn't like, but what I'll tell you on both of those trips Jasmine was smiling. At Disney World during the parade and the light show, she was smiling with excitement. Jasmine loves lights. For her to be in a situation where she was with her family and experiencing something she likes is something that I know she will remember. She is more visual than anything since she cannot hear. Jasmine goes by sight what she does remember. So yes, these trips were for both of us.

One thing I am thankful for is that I had the ability and opportunity to do these trips for her. So, any emotional stress I endured, is worth it even as Jasmine is now a special needs woman. I do not take any of this lightly. The Lord would never put more on you than you can bear. And, if it's something that you think you cannot endure, you can bear it. In other words, you can handle it.

Although, I got pregnant the first time I had sex and even though I never wanted any children, I do know that God gave Jasmine to me for a reason. It is Jasmine that is responsible for the woman that I am today, the mother that I am to her, and my bonus babies. I will share more about my bonus babies later. Each one gave me something that helped mold me into a responsible person. They each have taught me how to love in different ways.

Jasmine taught me how to be an advocate for her needs, not just medical requirements. I had to also maintain her educational files of what she needed on a regular basis over the last couple of decades. Her educational needs were just as important as her medical requirements.

So, as Jasmine's advocate, I had to and continue to advocate her needs. Today, I can say with certainty that my level of advocacy is on a *whole other level*, because of the knowledge and experience I have obtained. I know Jasmine's likes and dislikes. She is cared for and loved. I am thankful for Seguin. When Jasmine was aging out of her program, at the Little City Foundation. I thought she would not have anywhere else to go. I went to visit many facilities to see if they would be a perfect fit. I knew in my heart once I got there, these places were not suitable for Jasmine.

Seguin has done an amazing job of making sure that her needs are met, and I appreciate how they collaborate with me on Jasmine's needs. I know that the individuals that are responsible for caring for her that they don't make a lot of money, but they love what they do, and I know that they love Jasmine. And honestly, we've been so blessed to be able to utilize resources to make sure that her needs are met.

In 1995, Jasmine started off at the Blue Cap Center. And this is where I had my first experience with the IEP. It was there where a social worker came to me and said, "I think that Jasmine would benefit from a residential facility."

I'm blessed that Jasmine has made it to thirty-one with no trauma or situations happening to her. She is a tough cookie. Jasmine doesn't want anybody to touch her. My biggest fear was would someone try to sexually assault her.

I remember as a child experiencing some sexual inappropriateness. I have never shared this with anyone. This is my first-time making mention of it. I am lucky that it only happened once. It did not traumatize me. I remember the exact place and location. It was still inappropriate, and I do not want Jasmine to have this awful experience.

During this time, I had decided that Jasmine was going to be enrolled at the Phillip Brock Center in Glen Ellyn, Illinois. She stayed at the Phillip Rock Center until there was a recommendation that she needed to be in a different type of care. Honestly, looking back on it, I wonder what that different type of care really meant?

Jasmine had some behavioral issues. Primarily, because she cannot talk. She does not really use a full-blown sign language communication method and so I could see where it could be a little stressful to care for her now. I'll tell you today when I asked the staff about, you know, is Jasmine having any behaviors and they would say, "Please, Jasmine is fine." So that gives me a certain level of peace. Because working and traveling around the country is something that I must constantly consider. Is she okay? Nonetheless, we left the Phillip Rock school, and we went to Springfield, Illinois.

Springfield, Illinois is about two and a half hours from where we lived in the South suburbs of Chicago. Again, as Jasmine's advocate, her mother, I agreed to take her to Springfield. It was a challenge because it was far away. So far away, that if there was a situation where, if something happened or if there was a meeting, I would have to drive there.

My best friend Adriane, Jasmine's Godmother and I went to Springfield to bring Jasmine home for the holiday in 2007. While driving there, we entered a rainstorm. I told Adriane to pull over. She was determined to get Jasmine. Nothing would stand in her way. If it was me, I would have pulled under a viaduct until the storm subsided. But Adriane was determined. She acted like a hunter looking for fresh kill.

Adriane said, "We are going to get Jazzy and bring her home. God got this."

In May 2008, Jasmine was in a situation at the Hope School where she pulled her roommate out of bed. She has that only child syndrome. She wants her own space and that's it. And there was nothing you could say to tell her about it.

In June 2008, I decided to bring Jasmine closer to home. During this time, I was dating my high school sweetheart, Paul. He and I started chatting by phone and reconnected the same month and year.

A month later, I was heading to pick up Jasmine. Now one thing that you *must* know about hubby, he is an amazing father. And no matter what Jasmine needs, he got it. He is Jasmine's personal barber. Jasmine, you see, wears a very low haircut and Papa Paul always makes sure that her hair is nice and tight.

Paul went with me to pick her up in Springfield, and we then enrolled Jasmine in the Little City Foundation in Palatine, Illinois. The Little City Foundation was an amazing facility, and this is where I can say that Jasmine continued to blossom. This is where Jasmine, as I mentioned before, had the opportunity to attend prom. This facility had a prom every year.

My Grandfather, Edward Campbell Sr., and my Aunt Phyllis dropped Jasmine off at the prom. I am so blessed to have a supportive family.

My Grandfather is an amazing man. Today, at the time of me writing this book, he is one hundred and two years old. I know that I have longevity in my blood and there's so many different things that I want to do. I want to have an impact on everyone's life that I encounter.

Papa Paul and Auntie Phyllis were involved in moving Jasmine from Little City Foundation to Seguin, but we'll get to that in a little bit. So, at the Little City Foundation, Jasmine attended a program at a local school called the Kirk School. She continued blossoming there. Jasmine carried the lunch trays. She picked the trays up from the classroom and took them to the kitchen area.

One of the things that I've always advocated and always desired for Jasmine is that I wanted her to be as independent as possible. I didn't want her to be in a situation where she relied on others. Every time we had those individual sessions to plan her education, I always wanted to make sure that her goals were allowing her to be independent and grow and blossom.

Well, Jasmine had many wonderful years at Little City Foundation, and that was her residential facility, and her day program was at the Kirk School. It had gotten to a point where Jasmine was aging out and we had to look for an adult placement facility. She would be twenty-one and a half and it was rough trying to find a facility that was able to take her.

Seguin reviewed her paperwork, and they said they could make it happen and they did. And I'll never forget I was in the middle of traveling when it was time for Jasmine to move and this is when my Aunt Phyllis and Papa Paul took care of it for me. I am so, so blessed to have a support system that supported my endeavors.

I will tell you this, my Aunt Phyllis jokes about this all the time. Well, you were always strong-minded and independent, so there are some things that come with a different generational mindset. My family would often say I shouldn't do certain things and when I did accomplish it, they would make mention that they are glad I did. It really benefited me to have my own mind.

During Jasmine's transition from Little City Foundation to Sequin, her underwear was missing. This is an important point. Papa Paul said, "Don't worry, I will take care of everything." And he did. They moved Jasmine seamlessly.

Against my recommendation, the staff at Sequin put her in a room with someone else and quickly found out that Jasmine needed her own bedroom. When I think about raising a special needs daughter, I really think about all the things that I didn't know and all the different customs that I had to adjust to when Jasmine turned eighteen.

I had to apply for guardianship for her and the lawyer contacted her father and asked if he wanted to be joint guardian?

He said, "No."

I was not anticipating that he would say yes because he really wasn't in her life. I understand there was no playbook to refer to. I learned a lot by asking questions.

The advice that I would share with a family dealing with a special needs child is know your rights. Know the rights your loved ones have and do not take no for an answer. When your special needs child is in a situation where they cannot care for themselves, you are their advocate, and they need you to be their voice. They need you to be involved in their lives so that the folks that are caring for them will know, number one, that they can call you whenever your family member needs something. I believe they take a little bit better care when they know that you are that parent that really, truly is interested in collaborating and making sure that your loved one gets what they need.

COVID-19 happened. The pandemic hit, so we decided to bring Jasmine home in March 2020. Paul and I were visiting my uncle Michael in Maryland. At the time, the pandemic was being announced on the news. I said to my BAE, I call Paul BAE, we must go and get Jasmine. We decided to go to the grocery store and bought all the foods Jasmine likes. Her preference is soft foods. We got all the oatmeal, apple sauce and grape jelly we could find.

When Jasmine got home in March, we looked up and it was already September. This is during the time my other bonus baby Paul Jr. had finished his bachelor's degree and signed up for the Air Force and so he joined.

When I think back at that time, it reminded me of how I was able to assist Jasmine. She likes to sleep during the day and so at night Jasmine was up kicking it and so it was a struggle, but I was thankful. Over the years I had matured, I had grown. I had the means to be able to bring her home and still carry out all my duties as someone working in healthcare. I was able to do it, and I didn't miss a beat. This is a testament to how I did not become a victim of my circumstances. I became a victor. I know that I have grown emotionally and spiritually. As a result of raising a special needs daughter, I always wanted to ensure that I gave her the best life that I could, irrespective, of her disabilities.

Our pastor the late Bishop Willie James Campbell baptized Jasmine. I will never forget because hubby doesn't attend church. He says he is spiritual not religious. He and my family were there to see Jasmine get baptized. Bishop Campbell was delayed for some time because of a prior appointment, but the wait was well worth it. I will never forget my entire experience.

Being a member of St. James Ministries and the ability to bring Jasmine to church with me felt comforting. Our experience at another church was devastating. Jasmine had a horrible interaction with their daycare ministry. I never returned. I have only been a member of two churches my entire life. We ended up at St. James Ministries and that is where we found our church home.

At St. James, she was welcomed with open arms no matter her special needs. One time, in the middle of service, Jasmine walked up to the front with the choir and thought I should be there too. Bishop said to just leave her alone. She is all right. That really touched me in a way that I could never ever describe in words. It made me feel as if this was the greatest accomplishment, I have ever experienced caring for a special needs child. The doctorate degree did not come close to how this made me feel.

Wanting to expose Jasmine to some of my experiences are challenging at times. Such as going to restaurants. I'll never forget, one day Auntie Phyllis and I went to Olive Garden to be exact, and Jasmine knocked the seat down. She loves to eat but when she sits down at the table in her mind, she should eat right now and not a minute later.

Raising Jasmine taught me so many life skills and yes, I made mistakes, some that I will never share. But we came out of it on top. I am a witness that you can come from not knowing what to do and how to do it, to doing it well and being an example for others to really recognize and understand that they too can handle it.

My "Shed the Weight™" Moments:

1. There's nothing wrong with asking questions about what you don't know.
2. Requesting for help does not indicate a lack of strength or ability.
3. Research what you don't know, the more you know you will be better positioned to make decisions.
4. By researching what you are unfamiliar with, you can make better decisions with increased knowledge.
5. Never feel bad about removing yourself from a situation that is hazardous to your physical, emotional, or mental health.

Open your "GROW With Me™" journal and follow the prompts provided.

CHAPTER FOUR
The House The Campbells Built

Maebelle and Edward H. Campbell, Sr. are my paternal grandparents, my father's parents, who took me to church when I was younger at Lilydale Progressive Missionary Baptist Church. A partially dark to light orange brick cathedral architectural style building with vaulted ceilings and stained-glass windows which was built in 1913.

Now back in the day, as a young person, you did what you were told. My grandparents said we were going to church, and so I went. Now if you know anything about a Baptist Church, we didn't just go one day a week. We went twice a week including on Sundays. Early Sunday morning, we attended Sunday school, then we stayed for morning service. After morning service, we attended Baptist Training Union (BTU).

I don't think I realized the impact that The Campbells had on my life at such a young age. When I became an older adult, it has become crystal clear.

In 1983, I attended Lilydale primarily by arriving with my Grandmother Maebelle who was a part of the Gospel choir. My Grandmother loved to sing. Every time I came over to her house, I could hear her singing. I have taken on part of her character. From time to time, you can hear me singing at home. This drives Paul crazy. When he works my nerves, you might hear me singing even more.

The fond memory that I hold dear to my heart of attending Lilydale is being active in the church. Baptist Churches have disciplinary rules for their members from the youngest to the oldest. One rule I remember is that each member was asked to participate in an organization.

Raised in a foundation of obedience, I joined the usher board and the youth choir. On Sundays, I was responsible for being at my post whether it was on the usher board or in the choir stand before service started.

Once a week rehearsal was key to being in the choir. This prepared me to sing for Sunday morning service. The entire choir had to learn the words to the song, learn the notes in our part (soprano, alto, tenor, baritone, or bass and other singing voice types), and blend with the other voices of the choir.

On the usher board, we had rehearsal as well. There was a formal structure in place that the ushers must participate in during church services. When people arrived, we would instruct them to their seat. When the pastor is speaking to the congregation, we had to be in position. When it was time to raise the offering, we had to provide envelopes to members who needed one. Then during the offering service, we passed the baskets through rows so that members could give.

My Grandfather would say, if you're on time, you're late so when you're riding with him, you can guarantee that if the service starts at 11:00 AM, we will arrive by 10:30 AM.

Another fond memory I have at Lilydale were the speeches that I had learned and presented in front of the entire church. I had to memorize every word. Without a shadow of doubt, this prepared me to be a public speaker. While delivering my speech, if I made a mistake, somebody in the audience would say, "That's all-right baby, keep on going."

I carry these memories with me every day especially when I must speak publicly, I am nervous that I might forget what to say until I open my mouth then I remember.

We also had to attend conventions. The National Baptist Convention was an opportunity for me to experience traveling to other cities. Still today, I love to travel and take classes. This helped us connect with other parishioners of the same faith from across the country. The same level of discipline and structure were in place at the conventions. I realized as I have gotten older that I love structure. God wants things done decently and in order. This is who I am today.

I can remember during the services as a little girl, that the members were so emotional. The mothers of the church would be crying, and my grandmother, as some church members would say, *catch* the Holy Ghost instead of saying received. As I matured spiritually, I realized that those that were praising God had tapped into a higher power.

During one of the services, I had tapped into a higher power, so I decided that I wanted to become baptized just like my grandparents.

When I think back on my younger years, I can remember my grandparents interacting with one another. I always saw the care they demonstrated toward one another and how they treated others. The care that they showed toward others will be with me forever.

I firmly believe that it is their spiritual beliefs—their spiritual foundation that have allowed them to be married for seventy-three years, have six children, twelve grandchildren, and living to witness the birth of sixteen great grandchildren and one great-great grandchild.

This same faith allowed me to see my grandfather surpass the age of one hundred years old. Currently, he is one hundred and two as I mentioned previously, and yes, such a blessing. He is alive to tell the stories of his younger years and all the experiences he had as a young man courting my grandmother while being in the military. He would even share about the multiple jobs that he held. His stories are a testament of how his faith made him whole.

In addition to attending church, my grandparents also took care of the family. After school, we could look forward to a fresh home cooked meal. I oftentimes wonder if that was also a secret to longevity. They rarely ate out at a fast-food restaurant. I know that the lack of eating at restaurants was also attributed to having minimal resources with six children. This helped them control what was going into their bodies. I firmly believe that their healthy eating and faith contributed to the long life they experienced.

As I consider The House The Campbells Built, I am reminded of the six children that my grandparents gave birth to, three boys and three girls: Edward Jr. (my father), William, Michael, Beverly, Diane, and Phyllis.

Aunt Beverly is the oldest of the six children. She is a math genius. She would always challenge us to love math. I must admit that I really did not embrace math as much as she did. She became my resource that I could count on whenever I had a problem with understanding math. Her mathematical mind always kept us on our toes.

Every summer, I looked forward to going over to Aunt Beverly's home. She lived in the Englewood community and would always take us to fun town on 95th Street and Stony Island. We would go to water parks and every fourth of July would go to Navy Pier to see the fireworks. One of the characteristics of Aunt Beverly that I enjoyed the most is that she has a quirky humorous side about her.

She would always host the annual New Year's Day family gatherings. One thing we could count on was her serving healthy food. Aunt Beverly was health conscious and active woman who was in great shape because she loved to roller skate. Shortly after her seventieth birthday, she was diagnosed with Lewy body dementia. She would mention that all the years that she was so concerned about her body, God allowed something to happen to her mind. She remains in great spirits and loves visiting with friends and family.

<u>Auntie Diane</u>, who is the second oldest girl, is the nurse on the paternal side of my family. She will always have a special place in my heart. When I was sixteen years old, she made my dress for the cotillion on her sewing machine. I looked beautiful in my dress. It was a pure white ball gown that was fitted at the top of the dress full length that widened from the waist down. I had to wear long white gloves and pearls around my neck.

The cotillion is a formal affair where boys wear black tuxedos and girls dress in full white gowns. It taught me how to have respect and manners and we waltzed gracefully across the floor. The sense of dignity and prestige I received will be with me forever.

Now, Aunt Diane is also a singer. We would frequently hear her singing just like Grandmother Maebelle. She is the aunt that I mentioned earlier that let Jasmine and I move in with her until I got on my feet and moved into our own place.

<u>Auntie Phyllis</u> is everybody's favorite aunt. She never had any children and never married. She is the aunt that everybody calls on for everything. I could probably write an entire book about Auntie Phyllis. As you have previously read, over the years there are many life lessons that she taught me.

An inside joke is she was so adamant about making the bed with hospital corners. Although she woke me during the night, after she had gone skating, to teach me how to make the bed, I still till this day do not make my bed. As a little girl, I thought that was odd to wake me up during the night.

Auntie Phyllis, just like Auntie Beverly, was also an avid skater. She would skate seven days a week. This is how she balanced her life from working. Eventually, she purchased real estate. Just like my grandfather, she has a heart of gold!

When you hear me talk about The House The Campbells Built, that house being me, you can clearly see that I come from a long line of hard workers who are also intellectually unmatched.

I was my father <u>Edward Junior</u>'s first child—first daughter. One of the attributions to my father is my love of music. Believe it or not, Daddy still has eight tracks, a reel to reel, and an LP record player. You heard me clearly.

My running internal joke is one day I think those three items are going to pay off my student loan debt. In addition to my wit as well as my charm but most importantly is my ability to keep going despite what is happening. Case in point, my father had a stroke and kept working until he had another one then he was forced to stop working.

When people say to me you know you work too much, they don't realize that I come from a family of hard workers. My father worked for the post office for forty-five years, which is unheard of today. For my father to work at the same place for that length of time shows you the significance of my foundation and how I was brought up to stay committed and the meaning of stability.

The next child that my grandmother had is <u>Uncle William</u>. He is such a sweetheart. He is one of the kindest gentlest person you will ever meet. He is always willing to help and everything he does, he genuinely does it with a smile. When people see me smiling and say you are always smiling, I attributed that to my Uncle William.

Uncle William played a huge role in bringing us home from church. My grandfather had to stay after service because he was a deacon who was also on the Finance Committee who counted the tithes and offerings.

I blame Uncle William for my sweet tooth because after church, he would always take my sister Misty and I to the store to buy candy. Even till this day Uncle William still likes candy just as much as I do.

We joke about him being a sweetheart that is one-of-a-kind and that we are all one-of-a-kind, but his demeanor is 365 days a year. It is unheard of.

As I get older and I focus on improving my level of emotional intelligence, I see myself becoming a version of Uncle William. I already approach horrific situations calmly, which is a work in progress daily.

Last but certainly not least, the baby of the family, <u>Uncle Michael</u>. If you want to know about numbers, Uncle Michael is the accountant of the family. He is also the entrepreneur who travels and spent time in Spanish countries and is extremely fluent in Spanish.

Now Uncle Michael decided early on to leave home. We did not spend time together as much as I did with my father's other siblings. I did not get to know Uncle Michael until I was older. We spent some time together. I can remember one of his characteristics that we have in common is that he is a thinker. He is a procrastinator like all the rest of the Campbells and that's something that skipped me. I enjoy setting plans in motion and completing each of them.

Because he is a thinker, I contacted him for advice or to discuss business type deals. His conversation is very methodical, and I recognize that same trait in me.

The House The Campbells Built that I am speaking about started in 1973 when I was born but January 1998 there was another Campbell that entered my life, no familial connection to my grandparents Edward and Maybelle Campbell.

The house that this Campbell built was St James Ministries. Bishop Willie James Campbell, pastor and shepherd of St. James. When I first attended, it was located on 109th Street and Lowe in Chicago, Illinois, also known as the state temple.

I attended St. James with a young man who at the time I was dating. Our relationship did not work out, but I was able to experience church like I had never experienced before. This church which was a totally different experience than Lilydale Progressive Missionary Baptist Church.

Bishop Campbell was a world-renowned preacher. In fact, some might say he was a preaching machine. Others would say he was a praying man. When I attended and subsequently joined St. James, I was at a very fragile point in my life.

I had been broken and was several years into my healthcare career. I had just finished my bachelor's degree. In many ways,

I had lost my confidence. But, on Sunday mornings, it was something about the way Bishop Campbell prayed and preached with purpose, confidence and of course a sense of humor, that I came to realize that everything was going to be all right. Not only did I regain my confidence I began to grow and blossom into a woman that had been inside of me all along. This woman needed resuscitating.

You see, I had been broken because of young man who did not want to be in a relationship with me. My professional career was further along than he was. Nonetheless, I would not have met Bishop Campbell if it had not been for him. To put it in perspective, our relationship was based more on the present not the future. I believe he saw our relationship more as an opportunity.

My tenure at St. James gave me a chance to sing in the choir as well as lead the church health fair and other activities. My experience there was so positive that it gave me the fuel I needed to continue growing. Even though Bishop Campbell is no longer with us, his teachings and his prayers are carried with me in my heart. I am so thankful for YouTube because I can always press play and hear his voice. Thank you, Bishop Campbell.

Look deeper within yourself and find that person that needs to be resuscitated. You owe it to yourself to let the part of your past go that has been holding you back. It is time to walk forward anew.

My "Shed the Weight™" Moments:

1. Church taught me more than religion, I learned how to be disciplined, follow rules, and learned how to speak in front of large audiences.
2. Beyond religious teachings, attending church instilled in me the values of discipline, rule-following, and public speaking skills.
3. My existence is a testament to a legacy of dedication, perseverance, and affection.
4. It's acceptable to feel shattered, but crucial to acknowledge that the situation will not persist. With faith, seeking assistance, and continuing to progress, one can emerge victoriously from any circumstance.
5. Never, ever, lose your confidence!

Open your "GROW With Me™" journal and follow the prompts provided.

CHAPTER FIVE
You Work Too Much

If I had a dollar for every time, I heard the statement you work too much, I would be a billionaire. No matter what setting I'm in, no matter who I am with, I am constantly presented with these questions: "Are you working today? Are you still working? You're always working do you ever get any rest?"

The mere statement by itself really causes me to have to do some deep breathing because one part is I must stop and ask myself is the individual concerned about me or is this more about them. I know that in most cases people are really concerned about me. But I've also come to realize that many people have what I like to call *a nine to five mentality* and you know that's okay. My work ethic and what I do or how I do it, is not for everyone.

The other part is no one ever asks, "How can I help," *right*. They're so busy saying how hard I work, but no one ever asks, "Can I help you?" This goes with the statement that everyone is so quick to present a problem but not likely to provide a solution. The funny thing is I am the exact opposite. If I see someone has a lot going on, I am more than likely to jump in and help. As I have gotten older, I have resorted to saying, "Let me know if I can support you." As opposed to flat out offering to help.

When I was younger my aunt Phyllis and my grandmother Maebelle would often say you are hardheaded, and you don't listen. As I reflect on those statements as I get older in some instances, I absolutely could have listened. Such as my second car, a dodge neon, which was a demo car (only 5000 miles on it) and I paid 35% interest rate. Phyllis said that's insane, but I did it anyway.

But honestly in other situations, the decisions that I made were the best decisions for me. Ultimately, they were the right decisions. Oftentimes when individuals make recommendations to you, they make those recommendations not necessarily on what they have experienced, but maybe something that they have read. Today, Aunt Phyllis tells me how proud of me she is and today she remains one of my biggest supporters.

For instance, let's take my grandmother Maebelle who was an avid reader and recordkeeper. I realized today that I am a lot like her. To some extent, I'm not going to say she had a narrow-minded way of thinking, but her way of thinking was relegated to the time frame in which she was brought up and had experienced.

For example, when I purchased my first house, she made a comment that a single woman should not purchase a home alone. Well, I wasn't going to allow that statement to stop me from carrying out my dream.

GROW WITH ME

When I did my dissertation, I based it on lived experiences. So, what does that mean? I truly believe that what individuals have lived and experienced are the best resources to share. It is one thing to read how scary a roller-coaster is but another when we ride a roller-coaster.

Let me explain further, when individuals offer me advice about *you work too hard-do you ever take time to rest,* I often ask myself the question as to why you are spending precious moments you cannot get back worried about me. I understand that most are genuinely concerned. I also acknowledge that people can only make comments based on their lived experiences. If you've only lived a $40,000 a year experience, that's the only experience that you have. This is not my story. It's about the things that I want to leave for my legacy. It is about having resources to help those who are in need.

In 1989, I started working at McDonald's and I have been working ever since. My husband and I often joke about this. It is true; I don't think that I am ever going to retire. You may also be wondering why because isn't that the American dream to work, retire and then see the world. Well, I can tell you this that I personally absolutely enjoy what I am doing today. There is a saying that if you enjoy what you're doing, you never have to work a day in your life. While I am doing what I enjoy, I am also taking time to see the world. This way I do not have to wait until I retire.

An old school mindset and a traditional mindset when it comes to working, is an eight hour a day shift. You don't do anything before or after. My mindset is completely different for a variety of reasons. I've come to the realization that I do not owe anyone an explanation as to why I work so hard but let me share.

When I think about my number one reason for working, I consider my daughter Jasmine. When I die, she does not have any biological siblings to take care of her. Now, you may be thinking she has a stepbrother and two stepsisters who can take care of her. This may be true in a sense. Jasmine's life should not become a burden to those who have a life of their own plus she needs professional care. This type of care I must pay for and coordinate for her while I am here. Therefore, I come to realize that I must ensure that a Trust or some form of legal structure is in place to ensure that she has quality care. The same that she has been receiving.

Jasmine's current living situation today is that she lives in a community integrated living facility also known as a CILA. Technically she can stay there forever. The reality is there are many needs that she has that I handle and so the question that many people don't realize is what happens if I am not here?

In addition to that question and what's mindboggling are the questions that run through my mind, *are they going to take care of those needs for Jasmine? Do they even know what those needs are to take care of a special needs person? Are they even able to take care of her needs?*

Therefore, when individuals make the statement, you work so hard, they do not really know the root cause as to why I work so hard. Jasmine deserves to have quality care for as long as she lives, especially after me and my husband's life. I do not want to even put this responsibility on Paul after I am gone.

He and I both are providing support to our parents, and we understand the true meaning of caregiver.

Let me talk about the other reason as to why I wholeheartedly enjoy what I do. Many people are working their nine to five jobs. They either went to school to work in a particular field or have a job they've been working since high school, and they hate it. This is not my story.

I went to school for a healthcare related career, and I can honestly say that I enjoy every aspect of it. Every day of the week, I wake up thinking about *what else can I learn about healthcare that I have not learned? What additional training can I receive? What additional certifications can I obtain to continue to be one of the best in the field?* When I say that I enjoy what I do, I truly mean it. Not too many people can say this.

Think about those who have been working the same job since high school for thirty and forty years. They might express disappointment although they receive a pension. We might hear some saying, they are bored or depressed or not able to make ends meet. This makes us ask ourselves, is that the type of life we want – work and never becoming successful – leaving nothing for the next generation.

Speaking of generations, one of the reasons that I work so hard is about the future of the family. The things that we go through in life is not just about us. It is about those that we encounter. It is about having an impact on everyone that encounters us.

I recently asked several friends and family members to name three words that best describes me. One of the words which is a key theme that was mentioned is LEADER, another AUTHENTIC, and the other word is PASSIONATE.

The leadership quality is one that I have possessed since I was younger. I believe in being authentic and genuine because I want people to meet the real person, every time they encounter me. I have become passionate about my goals and successes. These three words are part of my demeanor – my make up. Others would not be able to describe me using these three words if I did not continue working so hard – working too much as they would say.

Because I am constantly challenging myself to do better and contrary to popular belief, I do know how to lie down when I feel myself getting tired. I do go to bed at a decent hour. Anyone who knows me knows that 9:00 PM is the time that I like to be in bed. I believe you can do more with a good night's sleep.

If you're reading this book and you are struggling with growing because you are listening to the noise around you, that noise being others that are in your life whether its friends or family, I say to you to consider what's in your heart. You must have an epiphany to suddenly believe and realize your destiny, path and commitment is yours to achieve.

If you started something and was unable to finish it, recommit yourself now to achieving every goal that you struggled accomplishing. The path you decide to take is the best path for you. Work consistently on achieving everything you set out to do. It may not be easy and might be challenging, but when you are focused no matter what, it will be well worth it.

Year after year – month after month – day after day, I see the growth in myself. I see the ability to impact the world. It's not about financial growth either. Yes. Financially, I have grown and have accomplished great things. My financial growth has contributed to me becoming a philanthropist. Donating to homeless and women's shelters and donating book bags for school aged children so working hard is not just for me. It is for others.

You too can become financially stable if you work hard, you will have more to give. Do not be confused, working more does give you resources but when you are doing it for the money, those thoughts get in the way. You begin measuring success based on money. When the money does not come in the way you think it should, you might give up too soon.

Let's discuss becoming what some would call a workaholic. I call it becoming my authentic self. This is a repeat of what I have already expressed before, but I want to make a point here. In 1989 I started working as a cashier at McDonald's. The reason why I started working at McDonald's was really to provide my mother with some financial relief in our household. She had become a single parent, and I believed that if I had a job, I could help her out in the household. Of course, that did allow me an opportunity to purchase my very first designer purse and gold bracelet. It also gave me a sense of accomplishment. It allowed me to understand that hard work truly does pay off.

While working as a cashier, I quickly realized that only being able to work the front counter was a limiting belief. It was limiting my hours and earning potential, so I found myself asking the individuals in the back how to cook the food. I found myself floating around the store learning the different aspects of the store operations.

After a few months, I was promoted to a crew chief. As a crew chief, I had an opportunity to train others, so anytime someone was hired, I trained them in their respective job. A few months later, I was promoted to a swing manager. As a swing manager, I was responsible for managing an entire shift under another manager.

Now one of the things about working as a swing manager I found interesting was that other employees wanted to work with me because I respected their position. I respected them as a person, and I was younger than them. I understood how they did their job. I acknowledged their growth and made sure that when the store was slow that they had an opportunity to float around and learn something new as I did. Shortly after that, I had an opportunity to become a shift manager.

My role as a shift manager allowed me to attend Hamburger University. In this role, I learned all aspects of managing the store from the front, the middle, and the back. I managed people and learned the resources that were available to serve customers with quality food and treat customers fairly with great customer service. Some might say well that was McDonald's. Or even ask a question, you learned all of that at McDonald's? Absolutely! I think oftentimes we devalue our experiences and think because it is McDonald's instead of looking at the true essence of what one has learned.

I was at a conference recently and someone made a statement, NO EXPERIENCE LEFT BEHIND. Everything that I do in life, I take that experience and I bring it forward which allows me to grow as a person. This is the reason why I can continue growing and enjoying what I am doing as opposed to waking up in the morning dreading what is next.

When you fast forward to the entrepreneurial journey, it really should be called a lonely journey because it truly is one where you feel all alone. You enter new territory that you have never been before. It is unprecedented territory. You might have to start from the bottom and then work your way up to learn all aspects of it.

I have been a director at a major public hospital and as a director, there are resources that are in place that I can leverage such as the Human Resources Department, Budget Department, etc. The Budget Department informs me of the amount that has been allocated for different functions. Based on the budget, I can consider future resources that may be available.

As an entrepreneur, one should have a budget in place to carry out the organizational mission. Being an employer verses an employee is a growth experience all by itself. There is a difference, and no one can really understand that experience but the ones who have lived it. Just because I see someone put on a size five pants do not mean I understand what it is like to put on a size five pants.

When I had an opportunity to be amongst other entrepreneurs that were going through the same lived experience that I went through – friends and family members saying they worked too hard, it helped me see that I was not alone. The funny thing is, everybody who stated that I worked too hard are the same people that want to brag on my achievements. These are the same people who never ask if they can help. They are here for the success not the journey.

Everyone has an opinion about what you can do to grow your business. In the back of my mind and sometimes I verbalize it, "Oh yeah! When was the last time you grew a business?" My favorite is "At my job, we do XYZ." I think to myself, *there is no comparison*! They will share where they read what Warren Buffet said or read about the Rockefellers and the Vanderbilts. Then I think, *let me know when I can read about your journey and your success and failures in business then you can share with me your lived experiences.* You're not the one that sees my tears; you're not the one that sees my pain and you certainly are not the one that carries my burdens from day-to-day so honestly, I don't want you to tell me about what you've read. I want you to tell me about what you experienced.

Back to this awesome group at the conference. I had an opportunity to join this mastermind community to be around like-minded individuals. To become a member, there is a membership fee. I would not be paying to be in this group because I got nothing else better to do. I am in this group because I have decided that I want to go to the next level. Going to the next level is up to me. The resources are there for everyone that joined but each one will have to have a desire to stick with it and reach the goals that are set.

I spent 48 hours with them. It changed my life forever. I literally spent probably two to three days crying because I finally felt like I was in a place where I could grow. I could bounce ideas off someone that would say, "You know what I think that's a great idea. I tried that as well, but you know what if you try this and use these resources, your idea will become successful."

Also, they directed me to the person who can get me there faster and will save me money. I have been looking for those who have lived the journey. I never heard about the books they read on the entrepreneurial journey. They directed me in multiple directions with options that I can take to propel me on my entrepreneurial journey.

I am already a speaker, and no one really shared about the amount I should charge to speak. When I look back on the decades of speaking, there were and I am not going to call them lost opportunities because my new motto is *no experience left behind*, I learned a lot from those experiences. Today when I speak, I will speak with a different approach. I will speak with a different pre-planned outcome.

Therefore, when someone says I work too hard, I will tell them "Grow with Me"! Watch me as I climb the ladder of success keeping my eyes on the goal not on the noise around me. Distractions will come and are meant to take me off course, but I will remain steadfast in my entrepreneurial journey.

My "Shed the Weight™" Moments:

1. It's all right if those who are dear to you fail to comprehend your vision. You need to keep moving forward, regardless of whether they understand, because you are the one with the vision, and they need not comprehend it.
2. At times, individuals may offer guidance without realizing that it reflects their own perspective and constraints.
3. Whether we act, the world will continue to evolve.
4. When the noise around you becomes too loud, it's time for you to move away so that you can focus.
5. Every experience, whether positive or negative, is intended to place you in a position that fosters personal development and progress.

Open your "GROW With Me™" journal and follow the prompts provided.

CHAPTER SIX
They Don't Know Me Or My Journey

From the moment corporate executives meet me in person, they are surprised that I was not the typical black woman. I am not the typical black woman because I am well-groomed. I can conjugate a verb and my outward exterior exudes confidence.

When I explain how I can help support their organizations, they become excited, and the journey begins. Shortly, thereafter, the dynamic of the relationship changes because they realize that not only am I confident, but I'm also well educated, highly experienced, and able to communicate with individuals at all levels of the organization. This excitement turns into intimidation.

Why do you have to list your eleven certifications on your signature line on your e-mail? Why not? Why do you walk around with your head held high? Why not? Why are you so excited when you stand in front of a room of physicians or non-physicians and discuss clinical documentation improvement? Why not? Why can't you act the way that we want you to act? Why can't you spend your day when you're on-site commiserating with us? Why are you so professional?

You see as a black woman I must be all the things that you believe I'm not. I must hold myself to a higher standard and more, the reality is I know who I am because I know where I've been. In high school, I worked my way up starting as a cashier and worked my way up to a manager.

When I entered healthcare, I started as a medical assistant and worked my way up as a director at a hospital and now president and CEO of my own company. I constantly remember that at age 18 I gave birth to a little girl who could not hear who the doctor said would not walk, who does not talk and who at age 31 is mentally about five years old.

Here are questions that I will answer in one statement:

- When you question why I add all my eleven certifications to my signature line on my e-mail,

- When you ask me why I hold my head up high when I walk down the hallway or when I walk down the street,

- Why do I always have a smile on my face, or

- Why am I so excited when I get to do and operate in my Zone of Genius.

It's because I'm happy of who my journey has allowed me to become.

What I have realized is that they were not happy about their journey. It's not my fault that they allowed themselves to become stagnant and focus on retirement. You see anyone that knows me understands that I enjoy and love what I do because I have a career. I have a doctorate degree in healthcare administration. I have a master's degree in healthcare administration. I have a master's degree in project management. I have eleven certifications in a variety of areas all related to healthcare because I realize my Zone of Genius, and I operate in my Zone of Genius. When you ask me why I do what I do and why I act the way I act and why I say the words and use the words that I do, my response to you is why aren't you?

Let me be clear about something. This book is not about Black, white or any other race it's about growth, so I think it's time for me to give you some of the tools and some of the examples of techniques that I've had to use when I almost threw in the towel.

- Resilience
- Social Skills
- Self-Compassion
- Patience
- Goal Setting
- Self-Care

In the next chapters, you will discover how I navigated through life using the bullet points above.

My "Shed the Weight™" Moments:

1. Education does not change how you feel about yourself. It gives you the courage and wisdom to be able to complete what you started.
2. Do not allow yourself to be a scapegoat for someone else's unhappiness.
3. It is necessary to close one door before another one can open.
4. Once you have exhausted all possible approaches in each situation, and still face opposition, it may be time to remove yourself from that circumstance.
5. Stay away from individuals who engage in psychological games against you and strive to continuously learn and improve yourself so that you stay ahead of them without their knowledge.

Open your "GROW With Me™" journal and follow the prompts provided.

CHAPTER SEVEN
Weight And The Wait

This chapter is about WEIGHT, not size per pound but about WAIT. Struggling with physical weight most of my adult life has made me realize something. I can stay stuck in a negative zone about my size, or I can do something about it.

When you are confident, others may view you as competition. Instead of collaborating with you, they can't WAIT to remove you from the equation. Here's the issue, what they don't realize is that when you remove a trailblazer from the equation, what you essentially do is disrupt the flow of something great.

So many people are angry and unhappy, and instead of being so consumed about why I had so many credentials on my signature line which coincidentally was one of the things that they were happy about—my diverse background in the healthcare eco system. Instead of being concerned about that, they decided that I was a threat to their position.

I started to feel a shift and that shift started to impact me internally, and that shift started to peel back layers of hidden confidence that I never knew existed. It allowed me to embark in areas of growth and motivation that I never knew I had a desire to do. The birth of The Growth Motivator trademark came from that shift. My coaching business, where I help others Shed the WEIGHT™ they've been carrying whether it is physical, mental, or emotional is impactful.

Now I'm not saying that I am an exercise physiologist. I am not saying that I am a personal trainer. I'm not saying that I am a social worker, a psychologist, or a psychiatrist, but what I am is a woman who has had to wait. Through my connections, I can most certainly support you in finding those resources.

During the process of waiting, there were times that I lost my way, but I never lost sight of who I was. Each defining moment in my life continued to allow me to grow. I experience the WAIT so many times, I lost count.

When you're on a journey to get the things that you desire, while you're in the waiting period while you're in the holding pattern, sometimes you *must* do the things that you don't want to do. If you want to get to the place where you want to go and, in this process, you feel a little uncomfortable and you know what that's okay.

I'm okay with feeling uncomfortable. I am not going to lie, it's a rough place to be. In the uncomfortable moments in my life, I lost sleep. I cried while on the peloton or treadmill. As I continued to grow, I realized that shedding WEIGHT while you WAIT is part of the process. Do I like it? No. I'm human so of course I don't like it, but do I like the reward. Yes. I like the reward so while I am in the period of waiting, I am preparing as I am writing my vision and making my vision plain. During my educational journey, in a strategic planning course, I learned about SMART Goals.

A SMART goal is a precise plan that is trackable objectively which stands for Specific, Measurable, Achievable, Relevant and Time-based. It can be used as a guide to reaching goals that are set.

I want to challenge you to consider creating a SMART goal plan and be sure to track your progress. Start with only one and accomplish it. You do not want to overwhelm yourself. Once you have accomplished this one, add another and another. See if you can focus on more than one at a time. If not, put the other one off until later.

Throughout this book, you have noticed that I had and still have goals set in mind. Some of the goals I set early on in life, I have accomplished. Being specific helped me stay focused. Next, I measured the criteria. When I want to start and complete a specific course, I examine what the course entails and how it aligns with my career, what it will costs, the length of the course, and how many days and hours per week do I have to block out on my calendar. I set reminders to alert me so that I will not miss it. This helps me dedicate myself to it.

Since I do not want to set unrealistic expectations that are unattainable, I set goals that are reachable. Although, there are times that the goals I set are beyond my understanding and somehow, I accomplish them. This happens when I do not realize the potential that I have within.

Nonetheless, as I mentioned before, I want to know about the lived experiences that others had on their journey. This way I will already have proof that the goal can be achieved and accomplished.

Although, I expect a lot from myself, I cannot expect others to be like me. I must see everyone as individuals that have many different expectations. This helps me to look within myself to align my goals with my values which are relevant to my purpose and long-term achievements.

Timing is also relevant to what I am trying to achieve. Some goals are reachable sooner than others. No matter what my goals are, the timing it may take to reach each are different. I still want to have a set deadline in place or a timeframe. This puts urgency in front of the goal which motivates me to achieve it.

An item that is on sale which has only a certain amount left, puts an urgency on it and motivates customers to purchase it before it runs out. I am making this analogy based on urgency, expectations, and motivation. Whatever it will take to accomplish the goal, I put one foot in front of the other.

Keep reading because you're *going to* walk away not only learning about what I endured during my 50 years of the WAIT, but you will begin to consider the WEIGHT that you need to get rid of while you're in the WAIT. That's going to take your growth to the next level that will allow you to be a happier person, that will make you more self-aware of who you are. It will help you improve your relationships because sometimes the dead WEIGHT that you are carrying is what's hurting you. It's not helping you.

I can recall dating a guy who was physically strong but was mentally weak. I wanted a relationship so bad, that I spent so much time WAITING to see what he was going to do about us having a relationship. At the end of the day, he was WEIGHT that was holding me back from being loved by someone that wanted to love me. As soon as he admitted that he didn't want a committed relationship with me, Paul came back in the picture after we hadn't seen one another for years!

There's a saying that you must close one door, before another one opens. I am here to tell you that you must Shed the Weight™ so that you can experience what's really for you. I've learned that what's for you, especially when it comes to matters of the heart are easy if it's meant to be! Don't get me wrong, relationships and marriage are hard, but if you are willing to put in the work and WAIT during the rough periods, you can persevere. Growing old together with someone else is not easy! That's another book!

We know when your BMI is high it's not good for your heart. Right? We got empirical data to support that but when you're carrying excess WEIGHT in the form of a toxic workplace, a toxic relationship whether it's a friendship, a church, a friend and all the things that don't mean you any good while you're in the WAIT that's your opportunity to clean the house.

Back in the day when I was growing up, spring break was called cleanup week for a reason. While you're in the WAIT, you need to have a little cleanup week. Because when you clear out all of the clutter, all of the excess WEIGHT, you can really see the path that's ahead of you, if you think about a room that's full of clothes that you're trying to find something to wear and versus a closet that's organized, I don't know about you but me I can get dressed faster when I can see what's ahead.

When you can't see what's ahead, you're like a hamster that's circling on a little wheel and you're not making any progress so as we go through this journey of getting rid of the WEIGHT while you are WAITING, take notes, reflect on what WEIGHT you got rid of and I'll share with you how I did the same. This is not a one-time process; it must occur during every season of your life.

My "Shed the Weight™" Moments:

1. WEIGHT is like the heaviness of a backpack that one carries on one's back, whereas WAIT is like the patience one must have when waiting for a bus to arrive at the stop.
2. Acquire an awareness of your triggers to recognize the tools and resources that can assist you.
3. It is better to have a team of resources rather than working in isolation.
4. Sometimes you need to strip down to the bare minimum so that you can regroup.
5. When situations don't go as planned, don't add more WEIGHT, just WAIT.

Open your "GROW With Me™" journal and follow the prompts provided.

Chapter Eight
The Village

There used to be a saying that it takes a village to raise a child, but I believe it also takes a sisterhood to raise a woman. As the older sister and as the oldest of four, I think to some extent I've always longed to have someone to look up to.

I've always been the one that motivated everyone else. I didn't realize until my late 40s how much of an impact that I had on the lives of people. The ones I knew intimately and those that I did not know. I also did not realize how much of a toll it took on my own life and to some extent how maybe it held me back or how it set me up for my blessing.

Let's just say that it took me 49 years to find a group of likeminded women that I could lean on, that I could cry with, that I could brainstorm with, that I could pray with and quite honestly that I wasn't the smartest person in the room, and I wasn't the most educated person in the room. I'm talking about my mastermind community.

But before there was a mastermind, I've had my village, my peeps!

1977 Misty

So, when I think about my village, my sisterhood, it started when my first biological sister Misty came along and quite naturally, she was the first person to ever challenge me to know Misty, is to love Misty. She will always keep you on your toes. You see she's a Slaughter woman at heart. She will always do what she's got to do morning, noon, and at night.

In chapter nine, I share more about Misty. Her tenacity to do what is necessary is a testament to her heritage.

1987 Genita

My next member of the village came during my elementary school years, and you know you never know who's *going to* come in your life and what impact they're going to have in your life, and I'll never forget meeting, interacting, and developing a lifelong friendship with Miss Genita. Till this day Genita I believe should have been an attorney because she can argue a case like no other. She will give you the facts of the case, the history and both views. You will not be able to get a word in edgewise, but we love her because she's the kindest person you will ever meet. In all aspects of the word kind, she's exactly like me because I'm a talker as well and just like her I'll give anyone the shirt off my back.

Now Genita is the one I spoke about earlier that would come by my house and wrap my hair. I believe in the 80s and it's still prevalent today because it's a form of a hairstyle that allows an African American woman to wrap your hair carefully and methodically at night so that in the morning it can unfold into a beautiful piece of art. Genita is also let's just say my Nevada buddy because she will kill me if I say anything else. I love you girl.

1994 Adriane

My sister from another mother, who is Jasmine's godmother AKA crybaby AKA applehead AKA bobblehead my best friend for life Adriane, who I spoke about earlier. We met at Robert Morris college. At the time, I was forced to retake my medical assistant program and yes, I said retake. Because the first for profit school that I went to had closed and because of that school closing, it was difficult for me to get a good paying job as a medical assistant. I returned to college at Robert Morris University where I met Adriane.

One day we were walking to the train station and as she puts it, "Who was this girl just a talking? Because everyone says Dr. Lisa L. Campbell was always talking."

Adriane is just like me. She has a kind heart and she's also a person who at the drop of a hat will cry. She is a crybaby and she's also a praying woman. Because during her tears she will quote a scripture. She'll be crying and praying at the same time much like me.

As strong as I am on the exterior there's a lot of times that I'm in my tub or in my car crying and praying or I'm praying and I'm crying depending on the day.

Adriane never had any biological children, but she loves and treats Jasmine just like her own henceforth the reason why she's her godmother and likewise Jasmine treats Adriane just like she is her mother. Jasmine also is not afraid to let anyone know and will jump in the car with Adriane at any given moment.

1998 Nurse Debbie

As I mentioned earlier, Nurse Debra has been in my life encouraging me for many years. What can I say that I haven't already said? She is a great role model. We developed a bond that cannot be broken. When we get together or even on the phone, we have so much to share. Just like me, she is also a talker.

Nurse Debra was also, just like me, very passionate about anything she was involved in. Oh yeah, there was that time that the school was in danger of losing its programmatic accreditation for the healthcare administration program and Nurse Debra immediately commandeered all of us students to get on the phones and call alumni to collect graduate surveys and perform any other tasks that were required to comply with any of the deficiencies that were needed to meet the outstanding accreditation requirements.

Additionally, we also decided that we needed to graduate quickly because we didn't know what the outcome was going to be. But the program did become reaccredited and in May of 2000, we graduated with our masters in healthcare administration and our sisterhood did not end. Over the years we have shared so many precious moments: the birth of her first grandchild, my first grandchild, her 50th birthday, my 50th birthday and my marriage to Paul.

I guess I should have been an attorney as well which was also one of my goals as a child, but I convinced Nurse Debra to join me at Capella University to pursue the doctorate in healthcare administration. Let's just say Nurse Debra and I are both lifelong learners. We have that in common and much more.

I started in the program May of 2004 and Nurse Debra started a few months later and in good Nurse Debra fashion, she finished much faster than me. I was grateful though because I needed her. I experienced several roadblocks in terms of failing one of my comprehensive examinations. It was her who supported me when I started falling apart and said, "baby you got this!"

I love her for that! She got me on track, and I went back the second time and successfully passed. After that several more roadblocks my God-given self-driven motivation helped me to persevere and complete the program in 2013.

Now our sisterhood continues to be strong today, and I must tell you Nurse Debra is one of the strongest women I know.

In 2020 she was diagnosed with a very aggressive form of cancer that nearly broke me down when she shared the news with me because the strongest person I knew, the person who was always holding everybody else down and fighting for everyone else to succeed, was now experiencing her own personal battle.

Instead of being the advocate she was the one who needed advocating. She was the one who needed the prayer warriors and the support system. Even during that time when the chemo made her sick, even when she didn't think she was going to make it. But guess what? All the seeds that she had sown over the years they came back in abundance because she had a village, a sisterhood that spanned across decades that came to her rescue even when she thought that she was not going to make it. I knew she would, and she did. We all had her back.

This happened to be the same exact time that I was going through the intake process for becoming a member of one of the greatest sisterhoods there is on this side of heaven while it is seen as the last sorority of the Divine Nine the Illustrious, the Greater women of Sigma Gamma Rho Sorority, Incorporated. On November 22, 2020, I became an official member of their sisterhood. Nurse Debra would eventually become my sorority sister, as part of Sigma Gamma Sorority, Inc. The first shall be last and the last shall be first!

I gained thousands of additional sisters. My village became bigger, stronger, and of course GREATER!

2004 Michelle

After obtaining my CPC certification, I started getting requests to conduct certification review courses from individuals, colleges, and healthcare systems. My first opportunity to hold a private class came from a powerhouse revenue cycle specialist. Michelle was as a director at Northwestern Memorial Hospital. This lady has got to be the smartest person I know! Over the years, we have developed a friendship that has been intact for 20 years. Our families have traveled together, we have witnessed each other experience so many life's challenges and I can always count on her for a good time!

2010 The Girlz

No village is complete without a traveling sisterhood and in 2010 I started to travel with a group of women. The first was Mother Yolanda. You already know her and the other was Mary, my mother's best friend AKA Booba AKA Auntie Mary. She is the cutest, the sweetest, the strongest, and most powerful woman I know. When she walks into a room, you know she's there. She is the life of the party.

Auntie Mary lives life to the fullest. She left Chicago for an exciting career with AT&T corporation, and she didn't look back. She loves hard, laughs even harder, and enjoys life to the fullest. She is well traveled so quite naturally as part of the traveling sisterhood. She was all too excited about commandeering.

Now next we had Michelle; she was the coordinator of most of our trips. Michelle would not let us go on a trip without having a minute-by-minute hour by hour written itinerary of every aspect of our trip and that included snack, outfits, hats, bags, T-shirts, calendars magnets and the like. Michelle was always the one who had way too much luggage that included but was not limited to shoes for every color clothing that was in her suitcase.

Michelle has been a part of our family for a very long time. Notice I said our family because Michelle is affectionately known by mom Yolanda as niece because fortunately mom met Michelle at CNA Insurance. Mary also worked at CNA Insurance and so Michelle not only was a part of the traveling sisterhood, but she was also around for all our life's major and minor events.

Our other traveling diva was Felicia, my healthcare sister in crime. I'm so proud of her because during our traveling adventures, I've seen her grow as a woman as a healthcare professional and during our travels, she left her job that wasn't allowing her the space and the opportunity to grow after 25 years all because she didn't have a degree. Guess what? She earned her bachelor's degree in healthcare management, and I'd like to think that I played a role in that. She also recently completed her master's degree because she desires to teach at the collegiate level. I'm pretty sure that I had something to do with that as well.

As I continue to understand the impact that I have on my sisterhood, my village, my community, I watched Felicia who as a young mother effortlessly raise her twin daughters and her son. I also saw her be an amazing grandmother to her grandsons actively involved in their academic and nonacademic activities including sports. Now that's a grandma. She exposed them to the travel bug also. Because as parents, you want to see your children and your children's children have more than what you have. Even though she was a young mother, she leads by example that you don't have to be a victim of your circumstances.

GROW WITH ME

I have traveled to 40 different areas in the United States. The 10 out of 50 states, I have not been to are:

    North Dakota

    South Dakota

    Idaho

    Delaware

    New Hampshire

    Wyoming

    Vermont

    Rhode Island

    Oregon

    Montana

Here are US territories that are included in my travel:

    Puerto Rico

    US Virgin Islands

    St. Croix

    14 Cruises (Since 2007)

    12 Carnival Cruise Lines

    2 Norwegian Cruise Lines

International Travel (Since 2002):

    Jamaica (favorite)

    Belize

    Bermuda

    Cuba

    Aruba

Dubai

Abu Dhabi

Canada

Mexico

Dominican Republic

Why wait to travel when you retire. Start with a group of family and friends and use a travel agency that can assist you in planning the vacation. You can always plan ahead for however long it takes to pay for it in full. Research online to see what to expect, although, it is totally different once you reach the destination. Keep track of the news about certain places to be sure it is safe to travel there. Order your passport in advance if you expect to travel internationally.

2013 Dr. Neisa

What can I say about this woman of God. She is the sweetest, strongest, and I know I've said that several times about several women, but every woman has the potential to be strong. Every individual has the potential to be strong, but I'm saying what I know based on what I've seen these individuals go through and my mission because of what I've gone through is to push others to their place – wherever or whatever that place is.

I met Dr. Neisa while teaching at a university full time online and we created an unbreakable bond in a virtual space. Years would go by before we saw each other in person and ever since then, we have participated in each other's major life events.

2015 Dr. Renita

One of the benefits of being a Health Information Management professional is that I have had the opportunity to meet so many powerful and strong women. It's not often that you meet a woman who is a Certified Coding Specialist-Physician Based (CCS-P) credential and holds a Ph.D. in healthcare administration just like you! Dr. Renita and I have shared so many life experiences, presented at national conferences and have co-taught courses at a university. She is one of my major supporters who has said for the last five years, they don't deserve you, it's time for you to move on!

2019 Temeka

I had vowed that my sister circle was complete, but one day, I interviewed Temeka for a course that I was staffing at a local college, and I felt like I was staring at myself in the mirror. Her teaching demonstration was flawless, and her energy was refreshing. If you ever have the opportunity to hear me speak, I hope you do, I bring the fire and so does Temeka. When you are operating in your Zone of Genius, you can teach others without batting an eye.

My "Shed the Weight™" Moments:

1. No matter what! Stay connected with a likeminded community you need support during the journey.
2. Sisterhood is not about blood, it's about a feeling that can't be established by DNA, it's through a common genuine goal.
3. You are stronger than you think you are!

4. Keep pushing until the end, you won't forgive yourself if you give up!
5. Your true village is easy; you don't have to work hard to connect!

Open your "GROW With Me™" journal and follow the prompts provided.

CHAPTER NINE
A Slaughter WOMAN

A Slaughter Woman is a force to be reckoned with, she says what she means, and means what she says! The Slaughter woman takes no prisoners and is always ready to defend her position. One unique characteristic of a Slaughter woman is her shapely lower legs. My Grandmother Ruby, my mother Yolanda, my sister Misty, and I all have this unique characteristic. You know how strong the trunk of a tree is that signifies the strength of a Slaughter woman.

For example, my sister Misty who like me gave birth to a baby at the hospital in Blue Island, Illinois who was born with special needs and this baby required her to demonstrate the type of strength that you can't read about, that you can't plan for, that you can't pay for, that you really have to be prayed into. I believe I know that it was The Campbells mixed with the Slaughters that allowed her to embark on the 20-year journey that she experienced with my oldest nephew.

When a woman is carrying a baby, she expects to have to care for her child when they're born. She expects to nurture the baby into an infant, into an adolescent, a young adult, and usher them into adulthood. Everyone's path doesn't go down that journey and us slaughter sisters got a big dose of *mama's baby, daddy's maybe*. That's what Mama used to say when we both experienced motherhood as a single parent, while raising special needs children.

Now my sister's journey in comparison to mine was similar but had major differences while Jasmine can walk and move around freely that wasn't the case for my nephew. I witnessed my sister carry my nephew on her hip and on her back. She too has those strong foundational legs as a Slaughter woman. Those legs came in handy because my sister for a long period of time had to carry her son, my nephew everywhere they went up and down the stairs back and forth to doctors' offices.

Now you may be thinking well that's a parent's job. It is but when the child is 50 pounds and you are 150, that load is a lot heavier than many are equipped to deal with. But a Slaughter woman, she's up for the challenge.

I remember as a young child watching my Grandmother Ruby operate in every space that had the luxury of meeting her and every person that had the privilege of being in her presence. Miss Ruby held her head high. When she entered a room, you knew she was there. She didn't have to utter a word. She was there with her stern looks. Miss Ruby was a looker. She was a fair skinned black African American woman and Miss Ruby didn't take no **** when Miss Ruby wanted something you **** sure better give it to her or there was hell to pay.

GROW WITH ME

Miss Ruby was a woman who was clear about her intentions. She loved to shop, and I must admit that I, like my mother Yolanda, have been bitten by the shopping bug. I remember when we would take my Grandmother Ruby to the shopping mall and Miss Ruby was very particular about which shopping mall she would frequent. If you took her somewhere where she didn't want to go, she wouldn't get out of the car. So, you might as well turn around and go where she told you she wanted you to go.

Miss Ruby also, back in the day, had white furniture with plastic covers. You remember those. You bet not drop anything on her furniture wrapped in plastic. Yes, the plastic because Miss Ruby had Spidey senses and she knew if you dropped something. Her house was able to withstand the white glove treatment even before it was such a thing.

Miss Ruby's house also smelled like mothballs. I never understood that concept of the mothballs. I just know I didn't like it but for whatever reason whatever room you walked into at Miss Ruby's house, you could smell mothballs. Notice I said Miss Ruby's house. My Grandfather, ASA II, affectionately known as June lived there too, he paid the bills, but he was a willing participant in The Miss Ruby Show.

Well, my hubby Paul wasn't around for The Miss Ruby Show; however, he has been able to be an active participant of "The Dr. Lisa Show," and he's still around so I guess it must be a box office hit.

Now something you got to understand about a Slaughter woman even though she's tough on the outside, she has a heart of gold on the inside. My younger cousin Amber is proof of that! She's a single mom, which seems to be a trend. But every time I see her, I am reminded of that Miss Ruby strength!

Miss Ruby had worked many years for the Department of Aging and so it's no surprise that the months leading up to my 50th birthday that I found myself on the board of directors for a nonprofit organization that provides resources to the aging population.

Look at your family and see the qualities that each one have. It is easy to look at the not so good qualities but find and focus on what makes your family unique and talk about how great they are when you see them.

My "Shed the Weight™" Moments:

1. I now understand why my legs are big and sturdy, it helps me maintain my physical strength, much like a tree that requires strong roots to stay upright.
2. Always be clear about your intentions.
3. My strength is built on over 100 years of suffering.
4. Just because you grew up following certain traditions, doesn't mean you have to adapt to them.
5. It's important to look your best, it makes you feel great, even if you are crying on the inside.

Open your "GROW With Me™" journal and follow the prompts provided.

CHAPTER TEN
The Birth of the Growth Motivator

I cannot take credit for the name "The Growth Motivator". My sister Dr. Renita helped me with the name, she is such a powerhouse in her own right! Even the motivator needs to be reminded of their impact.

Recently, I was looking at a LinkedIn post where a young lady said I was her mentor and had commented on how she was a doctoral candidate. She recently told me that she was on this journey because of me. I asked, "Why because of me?" She said that even though I didn't know you when you were going through your journey, I admire you. I admire how you are always positive no matter what you are going through even when you have situations that happened, you always see the positive in those situations.

I responded to her post that said she was a doctoral candidate. In my response, I indicated that the journey was not easy and that she needed to put her boxing gloves on, and that she needed to keep them on until she finished the journey. When I made that post for her, I was personally experiencing yet another challenge during my entrepreneurial journey.

I had to wonder how the person who was always encouraging everybody else continued to be so strong. So let me explain to you or let me explain to you why you look at me and you think that I'm this strong woman who has it all together. What you don't see is the woman who cries in the car when she is headed to her office. What you don't see is the woman who is in the tub taking a bath and she is crying. You don't see that side of me because that's not the side that happens very often. I release it when I need to let go. I Shed the Weight™!

I shared this with you because I want you to know that it's okay to cry. There have been a lot of times people think that you're weak if you cry, it is not a sign of weakness when I cry for me, it allows me to release the pain and the hurt that I am experiencing.

My best friend Adriane recently said to me, "Lisa Campbell, you know why you are so blessed? You're always willing to give of yourself for others. I never met somebody in my life that is always unselfishly giving of themselves. No matter how people treat you, you still smile."

I realize that I treat people how I want to be treated. I speak to people how I want to be spoken to. Now don't get me wrong if you talk to any student that I've ever had in the course that I've taught, they'll tell you that I give them tough love. I give them tough love because I want them to be successful. I want them to know that the world is not going to hold their hand.

GROW WITH ME

This chapter on motivation is really centered around the fact that life is going to happen, but resilience is key! As a person that has experienced many setbacks, I am telling you that you must keep fighting. I am capturing my motivational moment for you.

Although, I'm in the car with my husband crying profusely because I'm in a place right now where I'm hurting, I am releasing in a safe place. I'm hurting because every step I take, I feel like I get knocked down. But you know what? I'm a fighter. Over the past 30 years I have witnessed that every time I get knocked down, I'd get back up. I get back up and I get back up stronger.

I get back up with a renewed sense of purpose. I get back up with the ability to create something that someone else is not able to create. A lot of people and I think this is attributed to what the mainstream media would have us to believe is that we must be the people that we see on television, but it's clear to me that there is only one Oprah, Michael Jordan, Bill Gates, Tyler Perry, Elon Musk, Jeff Bezos, Warren Buffet, or Steve Jobs. But just like it's one of them, it's only one of you and you must take the time to find your Zone of Genius.

Let's take my home for example, everyone always comments on how nicely decorated it is, and I am not ashamed to say that I cannot take any credit for the look. I can't create the decor in my household, but I can create a video or create a course or create a program that can generate revenue to be able to purchase the decor in my home. In fact, I taught for a university full time for 10 years where I am 100% sure that my talents were responsible for making them millions of dollars.

My husband, Mr. HGTV, can create and visualize the decor in our home that makes our home look like it's straight out of a magazine but see that's his Zone of Genius.

You probably are wondering why I keep saying my unique Zone of Genius. This is where I'm the happiest. It's when I know that I am operating in a place of impact. I know I'm not good at math and so I don't try to do anything that has to do with math. I'm going to fail so why would I put myself in a situation where I got to be involved in math. That's not my Zone of Genius. It's not where I'm going to provide an excellent product.

I want to encourage you today to sit down and think about all the things that you do well. What are the things that you don't even have to put any energy and effort into doing? The things that people tell you that you're good at. Ask your friends and family what are the things that you do well. That's your Zone of Genius. Those are the things that you should be focusing on. Those are the things that you should be working on growing and getting better and better at as opposed to focusing on the things that you're not good at. You may be wasting your time on things that you have no interest in. You may become stuck. One year passes by and five years pass by and then 10 years pass by and you're miserable. Next it starts affecting not only you but those around you.

Stop holding that WEIGHT.

GROW WITH ME

My "Shed the Weight™" Moments:

1. It's Selfish to withhold your gifts from the world, there's someone that needs to hear from you.
2. There's only one of you, don't pattern yourself toward others, you will never be them, focus on being you!
3. Self-awareness is critical in relationship building, your authentic self is who they will respect if you know who you are.
4. Focus on growing your gifts.
5. When you stop growing, you are devaluing your worth.

Open your "GROW With Me™" journal and follow the prompts provided.

Chapter Eleven
The Growth Community

When I think back on why I am so strong, I realized that I was born with mental toughness. I am reminded that both of my grandfathers served during World War II. My uncle Asa III served during the Vietnam War. When I was born, Martin Luther King had been assassinated five years before. The wounds from slavery and discrimination were still very open. Despite it all, my childhood was normal, and as I entered the school system, I got to experience friendships and a community that expands beyond my biological family.

If you haven't figured it out by now, growth is a process, and it is one that cannot be accomplished alone. While a fair amount of my growth was experienced in times of pain, other parts of my growth were accomplished with a clearly thought-out plan. When I think back on the last 50 years, my growth community is deep and wide. As my grandfather would say, "The community (family) has love that runs from cheek to cheek and heart to heart!" I want to pay homage to my community because I want you to understand my growth journey and how individually and collectively, they have contributed to my enhancement.

1979

I've talked extensively about my family and close friends, but I have family that I met in elementary school, some of whom are still around today. My photographic memory has served me well over the years and these people and events are forever etched in my memory.

For example, Curtis, we attended kindergarten to high school together, basically because we grew up in the same neighborhood. I am certain that our church upbringings were a common denominator. It has been amazing to watch him grow into a man, husband, father and now a grandfather. I watched his love story unfold!

In 1998, when I joined St. James Ministries, he was a member and an active member of the radio choir. While he was quiet in elementary school, by the time we started Fenger High School, he found his voice.

I can recall one day our high school choir went to sing at Chicago Vocational high school. This also happened to be the first time I experienced gang-related opposition while on the bus returning home, a person threw a bottle at our bus as we were pulling off from the school.

Nonetheless, Curtis's voice I heard that day laid the foundation for the voice that we still hear today. As we continued to grow, so did his voice, and I was even blessed to attend the taping of his first project.

Curtis and his wife Delicia had their baby shower at my home in 2006. I didn't have any furniture in the living room, so it made for a perfect open party location! Curtis also sang at our wedding in 2012. To show you the connection, Genita (mentioned earlier), Curtis and I all attended the same elementary and high schools.

1984

I was introduced to airplane travel, having previously only traveled out of Chicago via car with parents, grandparents and aunts to Canton, Mississippi, and Raleigh, North Carolina. My mother promised that she was going to take us on a trip to Disney World. I was excited to experience another part of the United States. Mom said she was going to take us and when she received her income tax money we left.

In my 50 years of life, as I mentioned earlier, I've been under the pastorship of two significant pastors. One was the pastor who baptized me, Reverend Lawrence Mosley, Sr. when I was 13 years old. Pastor Mosley also gave the invocation at my eighth-grade graduation in 1987. His motto was "Determined to Live for Christ." Under his leadership, I learned more about how my talents will make room for me if I remain committed.

1986

The first year I met Paul, we both attended early involvement, which was designed to help us prepare for high school and we learned how to type on a typewriter.

1987

My freshman year of high school was the year I was given responsibility for taking attendance for my gym instructor Coach Brooks. We also shared the same birthday, which meant he understood me. Outside of the fact that I had proven I was a leader, I also didn't really want to participate in gym class, especially swimming!

Fun fact, I tried to learn how to swim in 2017 and all was going well until I had a muscle cramp while under water. I love being in water as evidenced by the many baths that I take each week. I can't wait until hubby has the bathroom remodeled, I am going to take a bath daily more than shower! Baths help me relax and experience a spa treatment at home.

1988

During my high school years, I actively participated in the gospel choir and the Modeling Club. I loved to put on nice clothes and walk the runway. I later learned that hubby loved to watch me, model. The Modeling Club allowed me to embrace my body type and hold my head up. I wasn't the smallest girl in the club, but my confidence was huge!

1989

As part of the Baptist religion, I had an opportunity to participate in a Cotillion, which is a ball, a celebration that young girls participate in which symbolizes growth and development. I was escorted by Pastor Mosely's son Lawrence, Jr. The ball was memorable and consisted of reciting speeches.

Larry and I also had the opportunity to sing. In a previous chapter, I mentioned one of my aunts made my dress.

Many people refer to me as bougie, and while that may be true, I am a girl from the southside of Chicago that had humble beginnings and was taught early in life the importance of being a classy lady and always carrying myself as one.

As I walk on stage today, physically, or virtually, I know that my earlier years prepared me to stand on stage, be humble and deliver. I am not perfect, but I always show up as my best self. I am my own biggest critic and I believe in providing an experience. One day soon, I am going to deliver a TED talk message, the world needs to experience me! This is also the first year, I started punching a time clock at McDonald's

1991

So many emotions! The first time I experienced sexual intercourse was the first time I got pregnant. It was shortly after prom night that I had this experience.

My prom was a blast, and I was fortunate to cover all my own expenses, I loved my teal dress from Madigan's, which closed the following year. My nails and makeup were done at Carson Pirie Scott. I believe that when you work hard, you deserve to treat yourself!

My Grandmother Ruby is responsible for this perspective. As I mentioned earlier, she loved to shop. She is also responsible for my love of hot tea.

1993

Music has always been a very important part of my life, when I spent those 12 months at Coahoma College, I was part of the gospel choir, I believe in so many ways, music keeps me sane. Whenever life gets rough, there's a song in my heart that allows me to release the burdens I am carrying. As I write this memoir, I realized that I've been shedding WEIGHT my entire life.

1994

After returning home from Coahoma College, I enrolled at Robert Morris College (RMC) At Robert Morris University, to complete the Medical Assistant program again and I finally started to blossom. My head was clear, and my path was primed and ready to execute. For the first time in a long time, I felt like life was moving again. When I enrolled at RMC my mindset was focused on growth.

1995

Somehow, for one semester, I found myself enrolled at Chicago State University to pursue nursing. Yes, again I blame my Auntie Lynette. She is an amazing nurse who contributed to my decision to continue my education!

While enrolled at Chicago State, I was introduced to the gospel choir! It was the choir that introduced me to my girl Hosanna and her daughter Zhane. Now Hosanna is the ultimate diva and Zhane became Jasmine's protector, even though she is two years younger than her.

It's through these two ladies, I learned the art of applying my makeup properly. Today, Zhane is a professional makeup artist (MUA). Paul and I witnessed Zhane's prom, baby shower, and marriage.

Hosanna is so strong, which is why her name is so appropriate for her. I've watched her support and save everyone else, and it is my prayer that God gives her the desires of her heart as she joins me soon in the land of 50.

Not only was I able to be a part of her marriage to my brother Marcus, a gentle calm spirit, except for that flower situation on their wedding day. Let's just say that Marcus is not to be played with.

This year, I also became a member of the American Association of Medical Assistants (AAMA).

1996

After months of studying, Adriane (BFF) and I passed the Certified Medical Assistant (CMA) examination. I had to motivate Adriane to study, but she always said, I am not taking this test more than once. The girl with the low ACT score passed a national examination. This goes to show you the importance of learning faster than you are growing.

As a lifelong learner, I am proof that when you get to where you are growing you must be ready, mentally, physically, and emotionally. As Bishop Campbell would say don't let your feet take you where your heart can't handle. At this point, I was struggling and winning at the same time. Life with Jasmine became challenging, and this is the year I started exploring the residential option. While I was continuing to pursue my education, my heart was heavy because I felt like I was failing as a mother and felt so alone.

1997

After attending school for medical assisting for the second time, I had an opportunity to meet some amazing young professionals. One of whom is a guy named Brian, who loves to brag about how good my PowerPoint and presentation skills were. While in my bachelor's program, I also started teaching and kept growing! I was even part of the debate team. Fun fact, I've always wanted to be an attorney.

I love researching, preparing, and delivering presentations to a wide variety of audiences. I want to be the sun that allows its light to shine on them, through me.

This is also the year, I became an auntie to my first nephew Tairay, rest in heaven nephew! No more pain, I know that you and Grandmothers Maebelle and Ruby, and Grandpa Asa II, Aunt Gloria, Rosie, and Uncle Asa III are having a great time. I know that you are watching over us.

1998

I started my master's degree at Governors State University, the place where I met Nurse Debra. My first semester, my instructor told me after grading one of my papers, "I don't know how you earned a bachelor's degree; you are a horrible writer." I was devastated!

I immediately started thinking back to the end of third grade when my mom was told that I was reading at a first-grade level. Just like third grade, I refused to be defeated, I sought help from the writing center. I learned that my writing was fine, appropriate considering my Chicago Public School (CPS) training and I just need some coaching to improve to write at the master's level.

While on the path of growth, you are going to experience others that don't understand the power that words have and the impact words have on a person's confidence. By this time, I had started attending St. James Church and was an emotional wreck.

As I reflect on my twenty-five years of teaching, I now understand how words can hurt a student. I strive to coach my students to be the best version of themselves. I want them to be successful, so I push them even when they don't want to be, most call it tough love, emphasis on the love part.

As usual, I found myself back to music via Floyd Wilkinson and Reach Out Ministries (ROM)! I attended a service at Fellowship Baptist church where Pastor Clay Evans, RIP was the pastor. I had attended a service with a musician I was dating at the time. I was in complete awe when this group of 50 young people hit the stage in skittles-colored shirts and sang the heavens open. As I watched them flawlessly deliver three musical selections, I said to myself, I must become of this community choir. Hosanna happened to be in this community already!

Ever since I laid eyes on this community, my soul has been ringing! That's a community secret and everyone knows that I am ready at any given minute to kick it off! At ROM, I met so many sisters and brothers, that I still communicate with today.

There was one young couple with children named Monica and Desmond who are very special to me. Desmond was one very few people that Jasmine would allow to cut her hair. Both Monica and Desmond are my Aries brother and sister.

1999

After joining St. James Ministries my family got even larger. I gained so many sisters and brothers, Rozina (James), Delicia (Curtis's wife), Tanya (husband Bernie), Harriet, Mahogany, Shirley (Jimmy, RIP), Keisha (Nicholas), Tenile (Clem), Tosha and Serena (these women can sing), Diane, Felicia, Samuel (my Aries brother) and last but certainly not least my brother Chris Taylor. I love all of you so much.

Chris, thank you for coming up with the title of this book. It's so appropriate and as soon as you said it on one Sunday afternoon, I took it and ran with it! I am so glad Paul gained another brother during this growth journey.

I know this list seems like I am writing an obituary, but it's a celebration of life, growth, and perseverance. I have watched my community grow personally and professionally! We went from being parents to grandparents and our family keeps growing! Most importantly to me, they have supported my growth! Prayed for and with me!

We all need a community! If you don't have one, connect with me via my Facebook Group, The Growth Motivator because we need to explore you finding a community where you can grow.

2000

I purchased my first home, and it was an amazing accomplishment for a 27-year-old at the time. My Grandmother Maebelle said that a single woman shouldn't buy a home alone, but I decided that it was time. Apartment living was causing a problem for me.

In the apartment building where I lived, consistent nightly parties with music louder than a concert, trash thrown down the garbage shoot with a match starting firers which caused nightly trips outside to the curb while the fire department investigated. Jasmine was not home that much, but when she was, I had to get her out of the apartment from the sixth floor, not taking the elevator was no fun.

This was also the year that I became a member of the American Health Information Management Association (AHIMA). As a member, I gained thousands of new growth community members, including but not limited to: Dwayne, William, Charles, Rhonda, Joni, Angelia, Angie, Lucy, Leah, Charniece, Marilyn, Ann, Chris W., Jennifer L., Meredith M., Dr. Hertenica, Dr. Kristyn, Dr. Michelle B., Dr. April, Dr. Tracey B.

2002

The year my entrepreneurial journey began, talk about resilience, endurance, and dedication. If I can be honest, my best year was during the pandemic which occurred decades later. But as you should see now, the WEIGHT is worth the WAIT! I had no clue what I was doing!

I created my first brand, Physician Practice Resources, Inc. after a physician asked me to help him solve some billing issues at his office in Park Forest, Illinois. Once I completed the work, he asked me how much he owed me, and I was hesitant to give a number, and to be honest I didn't know what that number should be.

According to the Bureau of Studies show that most small businesses fail within the first two years. I self-funded my business, and it has drained me financially because I believe in myself and my expertise.

My love for helping others also included hiring coders with minimal experience to give them an opportunity to grow and in the career path they have selected.

As an entrepreneur, I've struggled with my pricing structure believe it or not until 2022 when I finally realized after working with a coach that an organization could never pay me my worth, but they should pay me my rate and while everything is negotiable the value that I bring to a person, or an organization is unmeasurable. However, after having a great year during the pandemic, I finally figured out my rate and my rate is my rate point blank. And to be honest all it took was a mindset shift. When you truly embrace your worth, you realize that you determine the value. You must leverage the expertise. You are responsible for helping others see your worth.

2003

This is the year I earned my first medical coding certification as well as when I began my professional speaking career. Life was better again, and I felt like I could take on the world. At this time, I was giving back to the community and started teaching programs for social service agencies to residents of improvised neighborhoods. I taught women and men how to draw blood and perform electrocardiography.

I can recall one instance, where I would arrange them in a long row, 26 students who were partnered up and I told them, when I tap your back, collect the patient's blood. Yes, they were practicing on each other. Not only was this a successful initiative, so many lives were changed and these individuals' got jobs and were able to move out of the dangerous neighborhoods they lived in.

2004

I earned another coding credential and began to become a sought-after speaker! It's humbling. I have some organizations that invite me back year after year! For example, the American Academy of Professional Coders (AAPC) local chapter in Rockford, Illinois until this day ask me to present the annual CPT changes updates in December! This also happens to be the same time as Paul's birthday, but I think he has accepted or is tolerating that I plan to go with them to Rockford, Illinois every December, I love them and they love me, so it's a family tradition that I look forward to.

2005

Being the growth specialist I am, I sold my first house and purchased a larger one, yup I was still single. This time Grandmother Maebelle said, oh well you are still single. I loved this house because my father was five minutes away and one of my uncles lived next door. I was still single and needed support!

This was an extremely busy year as I was in year three of my tenure track position at a local college. I was close to the end of the tenure process, which was three years, when I was informed that my process would be extended for another year. I was the only full-time faculty member, and I was responsible for three programs: Medical Assisting, Medical Coding, and Medical Transcription.

These programs equally had decent enrollment with courses running day and night. I had several adjunct instructors working with me and I was overwhelmed and unsupported. I was falling apart at the seams. I was reporting to a dean who by the way was a nurse. I have a deep respect for nurses, but this nurse did not respect me, or my expertise and she knew nothing about any of the disciplines I was responsible for.

During this year, I was working hard to get the medical assistant and coding specialist program accredited simultaneously, by two different organizations, for programs that are totally different in their requirements, talking about an over-achiever, yup that's me!

The medical assistant program required a site visit, and the reviewer told me in the car while I was taking her to the airport that it was clear that I was holding down this entire operation and I needed resources and support. Both programs were approved! When it was over, I slept for several days and based on my mother's comments about my appearance, I knew what I had to do when I returned from break.

After all of that in 2005, I left that college because I was being disrespected and devalued. In fact, I resigned two months after purchasing a new home. I went to work for a small consulting firm, which taught me some valuable lessons about the business side of being a consultant.

2006

I shed the WEIGHT that was holding me hostage! I was too young to be stuck at an organization that did not value me or my expertise. Given all that I had been through with obtaining my education and advocating for Jasmine, there was no way that I wasn't going to embrace my self-worth! I had come too far to allow individuals that honestly did not value me to hold me back.

I possess innate talents, profound insights, visionary foresight, unparalleled innovation, and remarkable ingenuity that people eagerly seek and are willing to pay for! I am not bragging. Half the time, I am amazed at what I remember, what I have accomplished, and whom I have encouraged.

I nurture my talents by staying abreast of the new information that better my skills. Each were given to me as a blessing to share with others. So, I will continue to motivate any and every one that wants to listen!

2007

One of my highlights of this year was taking a cruise and I fell in love with the cruise life! You want to know why? Yes, I love this travel, but it's something about the peace that I feel while at sea. I'll admit, I've never seen the Titanic movie and don't plan on it, but when I am at sea, my sleep is peaceful. Often, I fall asleep on the balcony while reading a book.

You may be wondering why I brought this up. It's simple, the more you get to know yourself, the happier you will be on your growth journey. You must find what makes you tick inside so that your outer appearance shines through no matter what you are wearing or who you are with. Reading a book on the ship gives me great joy, I love to read while listening to the soft sounds of the ocean!

2008

During this year, I was working for a company that required me to travel to Oklahoma and New Mexico. I fell in love with Albuquerque, New Mexico. The town itself was peaceful, it wasn't fast paced like Chicago. I invited Hosanna down for a weekend and she enjoyed it and so did hubby. The mountains were so beautiful.

The vibe that I felt when I traveled there for three consecutive years gave me a change in my environment and allowed me to educate providers and coders about compliance and documentation improvement. This opportunity was afforded to me by my big brother William, who is also a coder.

2009

I unofficially became the mother of three more young children, all younger than Jasmine! I met Paul's three children, Raven, Paul jr. and Tiffany! It has been an amazing experience being their bonus mom. They each have a special place in my heart! During this year, I had an opportunity to take Raven homecoming dress shopping. Today Raven is an awesome cosmetologist.

Paul Jr., our only son. I have so many fond memories, from driving lessons to college tours, college graduation and the Air Force. Now he has made me a grandmother and mother-in-law!

Tiffany, AKA the diva, is walking in my footsteps having earned a bachelor's degree in health care administration and is wrapping up her second year in her post-graduation position.

We have enjoyed so many precious memories during our vacations and let's just say, cruising with Raven, followed by Paul Jr. and Tiffany left me with a lifetime of laughter. I am so thankful to have the opportunity to experience life with them, watching them grow! I know they are just getting started.

2013

As you already know, even though I collected my research data in 2008 and had a huge party in 2009. I officially completed my program this year. As I write and reflect on this journey, the first thing that comes to mind is resilience and how faith and growth stayed at the forefront of my life at this point. Resilience is a muscle that you must continue to develop.

2014-2019

There was a part of life where I was adjusting to become a wife, bonus mom and working harder than ever before! This book is only twelve chapters so you will have to wait for my next book, "Growing Together" to hear the rest.

2020

I never knew what it meant to be a part of a sisterhood. Yes, I have a biological sister, close friends that are my sisters, but this sisterhood is different. As a single parent, I did not go away to a four-year university. I chose nontraditional educational routes that allowed me to work and continue to support my family.

Becoming part of a Sorority was something that I've always wanted to do, but after attending a few events, I realized that I was busy, and the time wasn't right. Also, honestly, I didn't feel like I fit in. One day I went to an informational with Theta Chi Sigma, a chapter under Sigma Gamma Rho Sorority, Inc. and I felt at home. The love that this sisterhood shows is second to none

To my Sorors of Sigma Gamma Rho Sorority, Inc. I love you all from coast to coast! As I travel the highways and friendly skies, I see you! The sisterhood, scholarship, and service. Later this year, hubby and I are traveling with the Sorority to Ghana! Whoa, talk about excitement! To my chapter Sorors, Theta Chi Sigma, what I can say, is you ladies are the *bomb*! I mean, your expertise, professionalism, and dedication are second to none. Some of you all hold public offices, principals, educators (just like our founders), social workers, doctors, nurses, lawyers, and entrepreneurs, just to name a few.

Last and certainly not least G.I.F.T.E.D, AKA "The FAB 14" my class sisters, fall 2020, I love you all! This year, we turn three and I cannot wait to celebrate with you in Montego Bay, Jamaica.

2022

In November of this particular year, I joined my first mastermind community. I am now with a community of professionals that are doing or have achieved where my growth path is heading me next. Pastor Joel Osteen says, "If you are the smartest person in your community, you need a new one." I finally found mine!

Hey there, my dear reader, are you still taking notes? Have you noticed that I just keep growing and growing? When I joined the mastermind, I was challenged to find my niche, so I asked my friends and family to name three words that described me, here is what they said collectively:

Words that Describe Dr. Lisa L Campbell®

- Accomplished
- Accountable
- Achiever
- Amazing
- Ambitious
- Assertive
- Awesome
- Beautiful

- Blissful
- Brilliant
- Businesswoman
- Captivating
- Caring
- Committed
- Compassionate
- Confident
- Connected
- Considerate
- Consistent
- Courageous
- Dedicated
- Determined
- Diligent
- Disciplined
- Driven
- Dynamic
- Educated
- Educator
- Emotionally Intelligent
- Energetic
- Excellent
- Family person
- Fearless
- Focused
- Friend
- Friendly
- Funny
- Go-getter
- Hard-working
- Helpful
- Honorable
- Humble
- Innovator
- Inspirational
- Intelligent
- Kind
- Knowledgeable
- Leader
- Loving
- Mother
- Motivated
- Motivational
- Motivator
- Observant
- Optimistic
- Organized
- Outgoing
- Over-comer
- Passionate
- Perseveres
- Personable
- Productive
- Professional
- Protective
- Resilient
- Responsible
- Results driven
- Smart
- Steadfast
- Successful
- Tenacious
- Wife

My "Shed the Weight™" Moments:

1. Write down everything you try, learn, and grow!
2. It's okay to dream because they do become a reality.
3. Now is the time to operate in your Zone of Genius.

4. I was born into a strong foundation, without even realizing it.
5. You must water your dream so that it can keep growing.

Open your "GROW With Me™" journal and follow the prompts provided.

Chapter Twelve
Faith Over Fear

So, by now you are probably thinking that I finished carrying all the WEIGHT but in November 2022, I had an experience that caused me to come to terms with some weight that was heavy on my heart and spirit, that I needed to shed.

In July 2022, I read a book by Ashley Kirkwood called "Speak Your Way to Cash®." What excited me about the book was that it helped me answer a question that I've been trying to figure out for a long time as a healthcare consultant who focuses on clinical documentation improvement, medical coding, and provider education.

I had another consultant that said to me you're doing an awful lot of speaking engagements so are you a consultant or are you a speaker. I wrestled with this for a long time because I thought to myself why can't I be both. I realized that to some extent I allowed their limiting beliefs to become mine in that area, so I continued to grow my consulting business. I experienced some success and some failures but just like a woman who is versatile and desperately wants a baby I never gave birth to this medium size healthcare consulting practice that I worked so hard to create.

Now fast forward to November 2022, when I attended the Speak Your Way To Cash® Academy. I got in the room with other professional individuals who had the same educational background that I had not necessarily in my industry, but they had doctorate degrees, and they were lawyers, physicians, nurses, marketing executives, licensed therapists. Every one of us are experts in our own right. I sat there during this Academy, and I started to feel a shift in my belly.

You know by now that my one biological daughter Jasmine I gave birth to via a C-section, and I have three wonderful bonus babies. I am saying this to say, but somewhere in the back of my mind, I always wondered what it would be like to birth something that was bigger than me that would have a huge impact on millions of lives. And it was at that moment that I started to feel this shift in my spirit and the shift in my belly which was during the Academy.

In the spiritual sense during the academy, I became impregnated with possibilities that I never ever thought I could experience and so I joined my very first mastermind community. My mastermind brothers and sisters will tell you that I was the first one to join on that day and one of the main reasons that I was the first to join was because I felt like I was finally at home.

I had spent enough days and nights crying and tormenting myself over the journey that I was on. I grew weary trying to explain what it is, who it is I serve, and how I'm doing it with individuals whose mindset was about working 9:00 to 5:00. Don't get me wrong, there is nothing wrong with working 9:00 to 5:00.

I am here today standing on the shoulders of my grandparents, my parents, my aunts, and uncles who all worked 9:00 to 5:00 jobs. But for me I realized a long time ago that I had to ensure that when I leave this earth that I leave a legacy. I want to leave enough financial wealth for generations to come.

I want to give you two analogies. Many of you reading this book have given birth to a biological child with doctors and nurses or midwives present to assist you during the process. Some of you have become pregnant with visions that require a support system to assist with the birthing process and to take you to the next level. Well, I found this in the mastermind community. When I joined, this was the first time in my life that I became pregnant with possibilities with a fully supportive community who had had the same lived experiences as me!

There are many times in my life that I questioned God's path for me. The journey that he had me on, but it was during the Mastermind Academy that I got my test results that said congratulations you're pregnant.

The positive pregnancy test was just the beginning of being part of the mastermind community which afforded me an opportunity to have weekly prenatal visits and multiple midwives who in some shape form of fashion kept telling me when to push. Whether it was a conversation about a long or short form content or whether it was, you need to have qualifiers for those that want to work with you.

For the first time, I was pregnant with possibilities. I had a whole village that was going to see me through to the end and this time this pregnancy was different. I was no longer a single parent. Because December 2022, just one month after my first prenatal visit with coach Ashley, I was able to birth The Growth Motivator™. Month after a month I continued to have prenatal visits that included strategies to help ensure that I was gaining weight in all the right places. I was shedding weight in all the other places.

I realized that there was one big, gigantic WEIGHT that I had been carrying for over 10 years. The weight that I was carrying was building someone else's brand. It was building someone else's bank account while mine continued to remain the same and sometimes in the negative.

Heck let's be transparent. A lot of times negative because I continued to grow my brands which required me to run my business, work six part time jobs teaching online courses, and a full-time job also teaching online. So, when I tell you that I understand about carrying weight, I wasn't kidding.

I was carrying a lot of weight. Entrepreneurs will tell you that when you're trying to build your brand, there are some things that you *gotta* let go and you *gotta* let those things go so that you can grow.

It's no coincidence that the title of this book is "GROW With Me" because I've taken you on the journey where for the first 50 years of my life, I was growing. I was also unknowingly motivating others. When my brother Chris picked the title with me, I instantly realized how powerful it was.

Coincidentally, the prenatal visits continued on a weekly basis! There was something different about this pregnancy. Normally when you are pregnant in the natural sense, you have prenatal visits once a month where the doctor measures your weight and checks to make sure there's no protein in your urine, and they check for the fetal heart rate.

What I received was weekly prenatal visits to check my heart rate, to check my accountability against the process and every time I thought I hit a brick wall there was another midwife that kept saying PUSH. And so, I kept pushing and then there was another breakthrough.

March 2022, I attended Black Women Sell Live and by then I'm four months pregnant, during a four-month pregnancy that's when that heartbeat is strong and so my entrepreneur/speaker heartbeat was as strong as ever before. This baby was not going to be a baby that required me to figure things out alone, I had midwives that were supporting me as I continue to grow through my journey. I started to see the birth of The Growth Motivator™ while I'm still a healthcare professional. I continued with my prenatal visits.

This time I help individuals and organizations Shed the Weight™ that's been holding them hostage because one thing that I know when you are supporting others in their journey, they want social proof. When you're coaching them through their journey, they want to understand that you are the correct partner coaching and guiding them on their journey.

On April 1, 2023, I celebrated my 50th birthday with 150 guests consisting of family, sorority sisters, church friends, travel partners, my sisters, my friends, my brothers, and all my community that has watched me grow including the ones that said you work too much. Many of them have said *sis* we appreciate you for staying on your journey. We appreciate you for never wavering away from what you saw in your future. I mentioned earlier that my pastor's wife said you *gotta* trust God even when you can't trace Him.

Now it's the end of April 2023 and my mastermind community is in the Montego Bay area, and we are here for a retreat. We are the speakers, the entrepreneurs, the lawyers that have gathered to continue our mission to grow, build, lead, inspire and transform the world. Many of us didn't know what to expect during this retreat. By the end of it, the mission was accomplished. The vision was clear, and we left pregnant with more possibilities than we could have ever imagined.

As I continue in this pregnancy and wrapping up this Twelfth and final chapter of what's just the beginning and not the end of "GROW With Me," I believe that all things are possible if we believe and put in the work!

Many times, when I've gotten up to speak, I would say a simple prayer, "Lord, let the words of my mouth and the meditation of my heart be acceptable in thy sight." I know now more than ever that my path is clear now.

As I write these words, I want to show you how my journey is going. I've had some false starts and some false labor because during this pregnancy journey, I've experienced an opportunity to respond to a request for a proposal to provide medical coding services. I saw this as the opportunity to shed my biggest weight – the online job I was holding onto at a university.

Since I had been carrying this weight for the last 10 years, I didn't tell many people about this WEIGHT. For a long time, I didn't need to because it was online. My Zone of Genius was in operation without anyone micromanaging me, without feeling devalued, without feeling or seeing any microaggressions toward me.

As a strong educated African American woman, I find that others have become intimidated by what I have to offer. Then it happened but see this time I was prepared because I decided that I was done and so I started strategizing with my life partner.

Paul who didn't always understand the journey that I was on, but he always supported me. When he didn't understand the magnitude, the impact that we are going to have on the world, but it became clear on the day of my 50th birthday when we were being styled by Brandon, a professional stylist. We both could see the future of our existence.

He is part of my journey, and I am part of his. We are one on this journey. I consult him as he consults me because what we do will affect the other.

I saw the vision flash across as clear as a brand-new piece of crystal that sparkled as the sun's rays caused parts of it to appear as different colors. I see myself on a large stage speaking and out the corner of my eye, Paul is there cheering me on!

One of the things that I know without a shadow of doubt is that you need a team. Thank you, Attorney Chiquita Hall-Jackson, employment discrimination lawyer who wants you to blow the whistle if you are being treated unfairly at your place of employment. You can no longer be silent about what's happening to you because the longer you are silent the longer you allow the situation to persist, the weight gets heavier!

One of the things that we don't do very well as leaders in the African American community is focus on succession planning. I realized at my 50th masquerade ball, while watching Ashley Kirkwood and her husband Chris that I needed a team and guess what unbeknownst to me, I had been building the team all along!

My new stylist Brandon put me in colors that I would never select for myself, but as I was shedding my own weight, I was free to wear all things that he selected. I trusted him. I realized that I am a powerful bold woman of God who's here to transform lives across multiple generations, nationalities, cultures, and nations for years to come.

At 50, I am just getting started and this is the year where I've realized that my power stems from the situations that I've been going through. Each have made me strong mentally and physically.

Leah and Angie, my professional organization sisters called me chaos coordinator because of my ability to calm down the madness. I thank you for that title because this growth motivator is stronger than ever before.

For the first time in my life, I've started to experience labor pains. I know what it's like to be in labor because I felt my water breaking. When my water begins to break, I realize that it was because I was shedding weight. I've been doing a lot of crying, that included crying on the floor in my office.

I realize now that all of that crying that I was doing was because I was shedding my own weight. I was shedding the weight so that I could go into the last trimester of my process – the path to deliver a healthy baby. It was by no mistake, that I became a part of the Speak Your Way to Cash® Mastermind event because The Growth Motivator™ needed a midwife to usher her into recognizing that her Zone of Genius was there in the beginning. I just needed to shed the weight. The assistance helped me to be free to move about the country.

The Growth Motivator™ is well traveled. She's had multiple passports. She's been able to speak on multiple stages and receive sponsorship to speak on behalf of others. Now when she hits the stage, it's going to be about her. It's going to be about the impact that she's going to have on the world for decades and centuries to come.

It has been an honor and a privilege to present this journey "GROW With Me" to you. Our time together is not over! While writing this book, I've continued to grow my relationship with Paul and have started writing my second book, "Growing Together". Growth is a Vibe! Growth is designed to last forever!

My "Shed the Weight™" Moments:

1. When I failed to lean on God, he gave me signs that let me know that he is the author and finisher of my faith.
2. I've been faithful to those that I've served for salary and benefits. Now it's time for my name to be in the keynote speaker position.
3. It's okay to be fearful, but you have been trained and prepared, you are ready, don't overthink it.
4. Your experience, persistence, and faith will meet you at the door of your next phase, closed the door so that the new journey can begin.
5. Once you execute faith over fear, there is no need to look back, you got this!

Open your "GROW With Me™" journal and follow the prompts provided.

GROW WITH ME

BIOGRAPHY

Dr. Lisa L. Campbell®, also known as "The Growth Motivator™", is a nationally recognized speaker, coach, and mentor dedicated to empowering individuals and organizations to unlock their full potential and achieve personal and professional success. With a background in health care administration and health information management, Dr. Lisa is a leading authority in the field of personal and professional growth. Her passion for helping others grow and thrive has earned her recognition as a sought-after speaker, coach, and mentor, delivering powerful and transformative growth experiences to audiences across the country.

Dr. Lisa's unique approach to personal and professional growth is embodied in her "Shed the Weight™" framework, which combines expert guidance, practical strategies, and motivational insights to inspire and motivate individuals to act toward their desired outcomes. This framework has helped many individuals achieve their goals, unlock their full potential, and create the life they want. Dr. Lisa's ability to simplify complex material and make it relatable and fun has earned her a reputation as a captivating and influential speaker, and her unwavering commitment to education and empowering underserved communities has made a profound impact on the lives of many.

SPEAKING TOPICS:
- Mastering Critical Conversations
- Coaching and Delegating for Success
- Leading Virtual Teams
- Navigating New Leadership Roles
- Cultivating Accountability in Leadership
- Shifting Mindsets for Effective Leadership
- Mindful Leadership: Leading with Presence and Intention
- Embracing Change: A Growth Mindset Approach
- Inclusive Leadership: Shifting to a Diversity, Equity and Inclusion Mindset
- Authentic Leadership: Shifting to an Authenticity and Vulnerability Mindset
- Resilient Leadership: Shifting to a Resilience Mindset
- Ethical Leadership: Shifting to an Ethical Decision-Making Mindset
- Servant Leadership: Shifting to a Servant Mindset
- Adaptive Leadership: Shifting to an Agile Mindset
- Future-Focused Leadership: Shifting to a Visionary Mindset

CONTACT INFORMATION:

Dr. Lisa L Campbell, PhD
14701 Komar Ave, Suite 2
Midlothian, IL 60445

 drlisa@drlisalcampbell.org
 855-7DR-LISA (855-737-5472)

SYNPOSIS: GROW WITH ME

In the inspiring memoir, "GROW With Me," author Dr. Lisa L Campbell takes readers on a journey of personal growth, resilience, and self-discovery. Through a collection of captivating stories and heartfelt reflections, Dr. Lisa shares her experiences, triumphs, and lessons learned over the span of 50 years.

Each chapter of the book unravels a different aspect of Dr. Lisa's transformative journey. Dr. Lisa provides profound insights into the power of perseverance, determination, and the pursuit of personal growth.

In one chapter, she shares a heartwarming story of navigating motherhood with Jasmine, her only biological daughter who is deaf and mute, revealing the profound impact of empathy, communication, and human connection. Through this experience, Dr. Lisa learns valuable lessons that shape her perspective on life and the importance of understanding one another.

Another chapter in particular focuses on "The House The Campbells' Built" which is a metaphorical journey about family and her spiritual growth, symbolizing the resilience and personal growth that can be achieved by facing challenges head-on. Readers are inspired by her reflections on work-life balance, shedding light on the dangers of overworking and the transformative power of finding equilibrium.

Throughout the book, Dr. Lisa confronts misconceptions, societal expectations, and the weight of judgment. She courageously embraces her authentic self and inspires readers to do the same, recognizing that personal growth comes from staying true to oneself despite external pressures.

The significance of a supportive community is highlighted as Dr. Lisa shares stories of the positive impact of relationships and the role of a growth-oriented network. Readers are inspired to seek connection, support, and inspiration from those who uplift and empower them on their personal growth journeys.

Ultimately, the book culminates in the birth of The Growth Motivator™ within the author. Readers witness the defining moment when Dr. Lisa embraces her role as a catalyst for personal growth, dedicating the next 50 years to empowering individuals and fostering community growth.

Dr. Lisa overcomes fear through faith and courage, sharing her personal journey of faith development and the transformative power it holds in fostering personal growth and resilience.

"GROW With Me" concludes with a powerful reminder that personal growth is a lifelong journey. Readers are encouraged to embark on their own path of growth and transformation, knowing that they can shed emotional weight, embrace authenticity, seek support, and become the best version of themselves.

This memoir serves as an inspirational roadmap, guiding readers to unlock their potential, find their own growth community, and embark on a journey of personal growth and self-discovery. "GROW With Me" is an invitation to embrace resilience, face challenges head-on, and celebrate the transformative power of personal growth.

www.ingramcontent.com/pod-product-compliance
Lightning Source LLC
LaVergne TN
LVHW061547070526
838199LV00077B/6944